I0814187

The Johnson-Gilmor Cavalry Raid Around Baltimore, July 10-13, 1864

Eric J. Wittenberg

Savas Beatie
California

Library of Congress Cataloging-in-Publication Data

Names: Wittenberg, Eric J, author.
Title: The Johnson-Gilmor Cavalry Raid around Baltimore, July 10-13, 1864 / by Eric J Wittenberg.
Description: El Dorado Hills, CA : Savas Beatie, [2025] | Series: Savas beatie battles & leaders series | Includes bibliographical references and index. | Summary: "The Johnson-Gilmor Raid represents a multi-prong land and sea effort to free Confederate prisoners at Point Lookout in Maryland while Gen. Jubal Early's threatened Washington, D.C. during the summer of 1864. The timetable for the operation was a schedule nearly impossible to meet. The operation was a fascinating act of increasing desperation by the Confederate high command, and award-winning cavalry historian Eric J. Wittenberg presents the gripping story in detail for the first time in The Johnson-Gilmor Cavalry Raid around Baltimore, July 10-13, 1864"-- Provided by publisher.
Identifiers: LCCN 2023040294 | ISBN 9781611216196 (hardcover) | ISBN 9781940669618 (ebook)
Subjects: LCSH: Johnson-Gilmor Raid, Md., 1864. | Maryland--History--Civil War, 1861-1865--Campaigns. | Point Lookout Prison Camp for Confederates. | Confederate States of America. Army. Maryland Cavalry Battalion, 2nd. | Confederate States of America. Army. Johnson's Brigade. | United States--History--Civil War, 1861-1865--Campaigns. | Johnson, Bradley T. (Bradley Tyler), 1829-1903. | Gilmor, Harry, 1838-1883. | Lee, Robert E. (Robert Edward), 1807-1870.
Classification: LCC E476.66 .W58 2023 | DDC 973.7/71--dc22

First edition, first printing

Printed and bound in the United Kingdom

SB
Savas Beatie
989 Governor Drive, Suite 102,
El Dorado Hills, CA 95762
916-941-6896 / sales@savasbeatie.com / www.savasbeatie.com

BOOK #4 IN THE SAVAS BEATIE BATTLES & LEADERS SERIES

This work is respectfully dedicated to the memory of the brave soldiers of both sides who squared off during Jubal Early's advance on Washington, D.C., and in particular to the memory of those men who gave the last Full measure of their devotion along the way.

The military complex located on Point Lookout as it appeared in 1864. *Library of Congress*

Table of Contents

List of Maps

List of Illustrations

List of Illustrations (continued)

PREFACE

I BECAME interested in Jubal A. Early's July 1864 strike on Washington during my first visit to the Monocacy battlefield in the spring of 1992. In those days, there was no visitor's center and no interpretation on the battlefield other than the monuments erected by the veterans. I had to figure it out for myself. Learning about this fascinating little campaign became a priority for me.

I read everything that I could get my hands on—which was very little in those days. I wrote an article on the battle, my second publication on the Civil War, as a means of teaching myself the details of the battle. Writing about people and events has always helped me learn more about them.

Along the way, I learned about a fascinating sidebar to the campaign, something I had never heard before. When I mentioned it to others, I quickly learned that few of my acquaintances had heard of it, either. In the summer of 1864, Gen. Robert E. Lee helped devise a scheme to try and free nearly 15,000 Confederate prisoners of war being held at Camp Hoffman at Point Lookout, Maryland. The overcrowded prison camp sat on a narrow 15-mile-wide peninsula jutting into the Potomac River. Lee's scheme involved a combined amphibious landing and an overland expedition by a brigade of cavalry under Brig. Gen. Bradley T. Johnson of Maryland.

A second column of 150 troopers under Lt. Col. Harry Gilmor of the 2nd Maryland Cavalry Battalion would branch off to create mischief that included menacing Baltimore, raiding the Philadelphia, Baltimore & Wilmington Railroad, and destroying important bridges. President Jefferson Davis approved the plan and set the military machine in motion.

For a host of reasons, the bold scheme has been largely overlooked by history. When it is mentioned at all, it is relegated to a paragraph or two, or in some cases a brief chapter buried in a study of a much larger topic. My hope is that *The Johnson-Gilmor Cavalry Raid Around Baltimore, July 10-13, 1864* corrects this oversight.

Acknowledgments

I have many people to thank for their contributions. Sam Beeghley gathered important source material for me in Westminster, Maryland, which was visited by the raid. My friend and co-author David A. Powell obtained other primary source material for me, as did Kimberly Schwatka. Mark Wade, the go-to source for everything Confederate Maryland, delved into his substantial library to provide me with valuable source material. Once again, Edward Alexander has graced my work with his excellent maps, which only add to my ability to do this story justice, and Nancy Hale did a copy edit on the first galley.

When I fell ill, Jon-Erik Gilot stepped in and helped with a careful final reading and edit. This could not have been finished without him and the patience of my publisher. Thank you both!

This is my thirteenth book with Savas Beatie, which provides me with a wonderful outlet for my work. Special thanks to Theodore P. Savas and his staff for the opportunity and for making my work better. Ted's new Battles & Leaders of the Civil War Series is perfect for a work like this.

Finally, and as always, I am grateful to my wife, best friend, travel companion, and proofreader Susan Skilken Wittenberg, without whom none of this would be possible. Thank you for your unflagging support. I could not do what I do without you.

Chapter 1

The Point Lookout Prisoner of War Camp

POINT LOOKOUT is the southernmost tip of the peninsula formed by the confluence of the Potomac River and the Chesapeake Bay, located in St. Mary's County, Maryland. This narrow point of land juts into the Potomac River at a spot where the body of water is fifteen miles wide.

The place has a long history. Capt. John Smith, the famed English explorer who later became the first governor of the Jamestown Colony, landed there in 1608. Smith surveyed the area and reported his findings to the King of England, calling special attention to the lush countryside and abundant fisheries.[1]

The first permanent settlement in Maryland, St. Mary's City, was founded in 1634 not far from Point Lookout. Point Lookout became part of St. Michael's Manor, one of the primary holdings of Leonard Calvert, the leader of the new

1 Robert L. Loeffelbein, "Point Lookout Prison: The Truth Beneath the Ruins," *Maryland Magazine* (Spring 1982), 12.

colony of Maryland and its first proprietary governor. British forces raided it during the Revolutionary War. During the War of 1812 it received the name Point Lookout in recognition of the important role it played in monitoring the movements of British warships. Its capture by the British, who defeated outnumbered militia forces there, led to the burning of Washington—and the White House—in 1814. President James Madison and his secretary of war, John Armstrong, Jr., received heavy criticism for allowing Point Lookout to fall into British hands.[2]

The location became a popular vacation spot in the 1850s because of its sandy beaches and good fishing. A settlement of several hundred beach cottages and a lone hotel sprang up as a result. Wealthy men such as Cyrus B. McCormick, inventor of the threshing machine, and Roger B. Taney, the Chief Justice of the United States Supreme Court, owned cottages there.[3]

In 1857, William C. Johnson purchased 400 acres of land at Point Lookout to build a seaside resort, but he never completed the project due to financial difficulties. In 1862, Baltimore resident William H. Allen purchased the land from Johnson, knowing that the United States government was considering using the area for a hospital and a prisoner of war camp site. Johnson took back a mortgage and gladly rid himself of such a large financial burden. Allen hoped to make a profit by offering it to the War Department for use as a military hospital in July 1862. Given that local residents held strong secessionist sentiments, this was a daring ploy.[4]

2 Ibid.

3 Edwin W. Beitzel, *Point Lookout Prison Camp for Confederates* (Leonardtown, MD: St. Mary's Historical Society, 1983), 103.

4 Loeffelbein, "Point Lookout Prison," 12-13. Union soldiers occupied nearby Leonardtown Court House, the county seat, from 1861-1865, and

The heavy casualties suffered by the Union armies in the spring of 1862 necessitated the construction of new military hospitals, and Point Lookout seemed like an ideal location for one. In addition to its isolated location, there were plenty of fresh breezes and it had good access for shipping. Surgeon General William A. Hammond had the land inspected and on June 5, 1862, reported to Quartermaster General Montgomery Meigs that the existing structures could accommodate 1,500 men with plenty of room for expansion. The War Department purchased the land.[5]

Construction of the new hospital began under the supervision of Capt. L. C. Edwards. The facility had an extraordinary design intended to give patients the benefit of its open-air construction. The building closely resembled the spokes of a wagon wheel with sixteen wards extending out from the center hub. Each ward had thirty-six feet of open space between the other, allowing beneficial fresh air and sunshine to enter. When completed, the hospital had 1,400 beds for the wounded and the sick. In order to guard against the threat of fire, the hospital design included a 20,000-gallon water reservoir that could flood the hospital building if it became necessary to snuff a blaze.

A circular corridor about eight feet wide by 100 feet in circumference connected the wards. Four buildings in the shape of a cross, including a chapel, a kitchen, a library, and storage facilities, made up the central hub of the wheel. More than fifty other buildings sprang up to support the hospital, including surgeons' quarters, a smallpox isolation ward, the commandant's residence, the provost marshal's office, a

---

they arrested many locals for maintaining Southern sympathies, including a number of women, all of whom were housed at Lookout Point.

5 William A. Hammond to Montgomery Meigs, June 5, 1862, RG 112, War Records, Surgeon General's Office, Letter Book 31, National Archives and Records Administration, Washington, DC ("NARA").

WILLIAM A. HAMMOND

Surgeon General of the United States
and namesake of the Hammond General Hospital at Point Lookout.

Library of Congress

laundry facility, a bakery, and other similar structures. Hammond General Hospital received its first allotment of patients on August 17, 1862. A contingent of twenty-five Sisters of Charity from Baltimore arrived to help care for the sick men.[6]

* * *

By 1863, the War Department also had a great need for new prisoner of war camps. Until then, regular exchanges of prisoners were made pursuant to the Dix-Hill Cartel. This formal system, developed in July 1862, established protocols for conducting such exchanges and was named for Union Maj. Gen. John A. Dix and Confedcrate Maj. Gen. D. H. Hill, the officiers who negotiated its terms. Pursuant to the cartel, a scale was established to set equivalents for captured officers to be exchanged for fixed numbers of enlisted men based on the officer's rank; agents for each side were appointed to conduct those exchanges.[7]

The cartel broke down when the Confederacy classified African-American prisoners as runaway slaves and not as soldiers. President Abraham Lincoln issued General Orders 252 on July 30, 1863, suspending the cartel until the Confederate government changed that policy and treated black soldiers the same as white soldiers. Northern prison camps quickly filled to capacity.[8]

6 Richard H. Triebe, *Point Lookout Prison Camp and Hospital: The North's Largest Civil War Prison* (Middletown, DE: Coastal Books, 2014), 11-12.

7 The War of the Rebellion: *A Compilation of the Official Records of the Union and Confederate Armies*, 128 vols. (Washington, DC: United States Government Printing Office, 1889), Series II, vol. 4, 266, hereafter cited as *OR*. All references are to Series I unless otherwise indicated.

8 Roy Basler, ed., *The Collected Works of Abraham Lincoln*, 9 vols. (New Brunswick, NJ: Rutgers University Press, 1953-1955), 6:357.

COLONEL WILLIAM HOFFMAN

Commissary of Prisoners for the U.S. Army and the namesake of Camp Hoffman prisoner of war camp at Point Lookout. *USAHEC*

Construction of the prison camp commenced about the same time as construction of the hospital. The camp was named Camp Hoffman, after Col. William Hoffman, the Commissary General of Prisoners for the U. S. Army. It was designed to hold 10,000 men. Gilman Marston, a brigadier general, was assigned to be the camp's first commandant.[9]

9 Ezra J. Warner, *Generals in Blue: Lives of the Union Commanders* (Baton Rouge: Louisiana State University,1964), 312.

GILMAN MARSTON

The first commander of Camp Hoffman.

Library of Congress

Marston was born on August 20, 1811 at Orford, New Hampshire, raised on a farm, and taught school to finance his education at Dartmouth. He graduated from Harvard Law School in 1840 and practiced law in Exeter, New Hampshire before being elected to the state legislature in 1846. He would go on to win reelection a dozen times through 1889, serve at two state constitutional conventions, and sit in the U. S. Congress three times (from 1859-1863 and 1865-1867). He was offered an appointment as governor of the Idaho Territory in 1870, but refused and served instead as U.S. Senator for four months in 1889.

The lawyer-politician also played a major role in the war. In May and June 1861 Marston recruited the 2nd New Hampshire and led it at Bull Run that July. During the Peninsula Campaign of 1862 his regiment was part of Joe Hooker's division, and at Fredericksburg was assigned to Maj. Gen. Daniel E. Sickles' division. Marston was promoted to brigadier general that November 29, but was relieved of duty prior to Chancellorsville and ordered to report to Maj. Gen. Samuel P. Heintzelman, the commander of the defenses of Washington, D.C. It was after the Battle of Gettysburg that Marston assumed command at Point Lookout, a position he would hold until the spring of 1864.[10]

By the third week of August 1862, Hoffman (the commissary of prisoners) had sent 1,300 Confederate and political prisoners to Point Lookout. The stockade was still incomplete by the time these men arrived; guards armed with bayonets on their rifle-muskets formed a human wall to keep the prisoners inside. Despite these crude arrangements, and probably because of the camp's remote location at the end of a peninsula surrounded on three sides by water, only a handful of men tried to escape. None of them did so successfully.[11]

10 Marston's wartime service did not end at Point Lookout. Just prior to the 1864 Overland Campaign, he took command of a brigade in the XVIII Corps of the Army of the James and participated in the unsuccessful attacks at Cold Harbor in June. After light duty in eastern Virginia and a receipt of thanks from the New Hampshire legislature, Marston did routine duty until his resignation soon after Appomattox. He died on July 3, 1890, and is buried in Exeter, New Hampshire. Warner, *Generals in Blue*, 312.

11 Beitzel, *Point Lookout Prison Camp*, 21.

Eventually, a twelve-foot tall stockade enclosed an area of about twenty-three acres. Guards walked their posts on a platform outside the stockade wall, with each guard post located forty feet apart, with a shelter every 100 or so feet to duck under in case of rain. A six-inch trench marked the deadline fifteen feet inside the wall. No one dared approach the line for fear of being shot. The camp was laid out into ten streets, each twenty feet wide, lined on either side by tents. The prison population was split into ten divisions, with ten companies per division. Each company consisted of 100 men, meaning each division consisted of 1,000.

As the camp's population swelled with the end of the exchange cartel, additional companies and divisions were formed. One Union sergeant commanded each division, with two Confederate sergeants in command of each company. The Company Sergeant called the roll, made sure the prisoners kept their surroundings tidy, and reported any men who were in the hospital or otherwise missing. The other was a Sick Sergeant, who, after morning roll call reported which prisoners were sick and drew the rations for those too ill to walk to the cook house.[12]

The prisoners lived in old Army tents that had been cast off after use in the field, meaning Point Lookout was the only Union prison camp that housed its prisoners in tents year-round. The unfortunate result was constant exposure to the elements.[13]

"We were put in Sibley tents, which were round with a pole extending from the top to an iron tripod, the pole fitting in the top of the tripod," described former prisoner B. T.

12 Triebe, *Point Lookout Prison Camp and Hospital*, 19-24.

13 The original plans for the camp included wooden barracks, but Secretary of War Edwin M. Stanton rejected the plan, insisting that the prisoners should instead be housed in castoff tents. Stanton never stated the reasons behind his decision.

Holliday. "These tents had been used by the army and had seen so much service that they would leak and we spent a very uncomfortable time."[14]

"Our tents were miserable affairs, being full of holes and very rotten," confirmed another former prisoner named James T. Wells. "They were of the Sibley pattern and into each one of these 16 men were crowded. In order to lay down at night, the men were compelled to lay so close together as to exclude sleep."[15]

The tents had a diameter of eighteen feet, and as many as eighteen men occupied each one. "We were packed like sardines in a box," recalled Holliday. "When we wanted to turn over in the night, the signal was given to turn, and all made the turn from necessity."[16]

On February 26, 1864, a detachment of 753 soldiers from the 36th U. S. Colored Infantry—all of them African-American soldiers—began doing guard duty at Camp Hoffman. These men replaced white soldiers who were returned to duty with the Army of the Potomac. "It was a bitter pill for Southern men to swallow and we felt the insult keenly," admitted Holliday. "They were impudent and tyrannical and the prisoners had to submit to many indignities."[17]

As Holliday later observed, the white prisoners resented being guarded by former slaves and did not hesitate to say so. The hostility of the black soldiers, in turn, was understandable given their circumstances in life thus far,

14 B. T. Holliday, "Account of My Capture," Special Collections, Alderman Library, University of Virginia, Charlottesville, Virginia.

15 James T. Wells, "Prison Experience," *Southern Historical Society Papers*, 52 vols. (Richmond: Southern Historical Society, 1902), 7:327.

16 Holliday, "Account of My Capture."

17 Ibid.

and their current duty assignment. As they often told the Confederate prisoners, "The bottom rail is now on the top."[18]

The addition of the black soldiers acting as guards only added insult to injury for the prisoners. On July 1, 661 green troopers of the 5th Massachusetts Dismounted Cavalry (Colored) relieved the 36th U.S.C.T., which in turn reported for duty in the field. These men of the 5th regiment were inexperienced and their camp was established outside the perimeter of the stockade in a vulnerable and isolated position, leaving them exposed should an attempt be made to liberate the prisoners.

The influx of prisoners brought smallpox to the camp, along with chronic diarrhea, dysentery, typhoid fever, typhus, scurvy, and all sorts of skin rashes, all of which were common in prison camps of that era. In 1866, Secretary of War Edwin Stanton would report that the death rate at Lookout Point was 25%, although more recent figures indicate a much lower death rate of 6.7%.[19]

* * *

By the spring of 1864 the command structure around Point Lookout was in flux. When the prison camp first opened it fell within the jurisdiction of Maj. Gen. Benjamin F. Butler, the commander of the Department of Virginia and North Carolina with headquarters at Fortress Monroe in Virginia. In late April of 1864, Brig. Gen. Edward Winslow Hincks, the

18 Bradley M. Gottfried and Linda I. Gottfried, *Hell Comes to Southern Maryland: The Story of Point Lookout Prison and Hammond General Hospital* (Fairfield, PA: Turning Point Publishing, 2018), 74.

19 Loeffelbein, "Point Lookout Prison, 12, 14. The precise number is not known, but it is believed that 3,000-4,000 prisoners died there. For an exhaustive history of life in Camp Hoffman, see Triebe, *Point Lookout Prison Camp and Hospital.*

EDWARD W. HINCKS, brigadier general, was Benjamin Butler's choice to serve as the second commander of Camp Hoffman.

Library of Congress

commander in charge of the District of St. Mary's headquartered at Point Lookout, was transferred to serve with Maj. Gen. William F. Smith's XVIII Corps of the Army of the James. Colonel Alonzo G. Draper replaced Hincks. Draper was promoted to brigade command that June, so Butler reassigned Hincks to command at Point Lookout on June 30. The merry-go-round command changed again in early July when Point Lookout was transferred out of the Department of Virginia and North Carolina and assigned to the District of Washington.[20]

Secretary Stanton, meanwhile, against the wishes of General Butler, decided to replace Hincks with Brig. Gen. James Barnes. The West Point graduate was a classmate of Robert E. Lee who had been lightly wounded commanding a V Corps division at Gettysburg. Barnes was not yet ready to return to duty in the field, so the camp seemed like a good spot to drop him while he finished recuperating.[21]

20 Hincks had been badly wounded at Antietam on September 17, 1862, and was just returning to duty in the field for the first time when Butler ordered him to report to Smith.

21 Warner, *Generals in Blue*, 20-21.

James Barnes was born in Boston, Massachusetts on December 28, 1801. He graduated from the Boston Latin School and eventually secured an appointment to West Point. He graduated with Lee in the class of 1829 a few slots below him in the 5th position. The engineer served as an instructor at West Point until he left the Army in 1836 to work as a civil engineer for railroads in New York, Massachusetts, Virginia, North Carolina, and in the Midwest. Barnes found it intolerable to sit on the sidelines with civil war breaking out and was appointed colonel of the 18th Massachusetts in July 1861.

Barnes served well with the Army of the Potomac in the Washington defenses and in the field during the 1862 Peninsula Campaign. He led a brigade at Antictam, earned a brigadier's rank that November, and fought at Fredericksburg and Chancellorsville leading a brigade in Morell's division of the V Corps. He was temporarily placed in command of a division after Chancellorsville, but did not perform well at Gettysburg at that level, where he seems to have lost control of his troops. As noted earlier, he was wounded during the Pennsylvania battle and although not fully ready for the field, was assigned to garrison and prison duty. Unbeknownst to Barnes, he would remain there for the balance of the war.[22]

Ben Butler's protests notwithstanding, James Barnes arrived at Point Lookout on July 6. Hincks, who was unaware of the unfolding command situation and ailing from illness and wounds of his own, arrived at Point Lookout the next day

22 On March 13, 1865, Barnes was breveted major general of volunteers for "Meritorious Service during the Rebellion" and mustered out of service the following year. In 1868, he was appointed to a commission to investigate the building of the Union Pacific Railroad and telegraph line. He died in Springfield, Massachusetts, on February 12, 1869, and was buried in Springfield Cemetery. Warner, *Generals in Blue*, 21.

BRIGADIER GENERAL JAMES BARNES

His Gettysburg wound was a chance to shuttle Barnes into prison service while he recovered. He was the commander at Camp Hoffman during the Johnson-Gilmor Raid.

USAHEC

only to receive orders to report back to the nation's capital for duty in the adjutant general's office. Because his various ailments, Hincks would also never serve in the field again.[23]

23 See *OR* 33, 1930-931; 37, 1:163-167; 40, 2:540, 597; and 3:18, 30, 59, 70-71.

By the summer of 1864, about a year after the prisoner exchange cartel had ended, nearly 15,000 men occupied the POW pen, earning Camp Hoffman the unhappy title of "the Andersonville of the North." The fortifications around Hoffman were still not completed, which only complicated the task of the small detachment of inexperienced black troops assigned to defend the thousands of prisoners.[24]

The camp's fluctuating command structure, limited fortifications, and inexperienced guards, coupled with General Barnes' fragile health, made for a potentially toxic combination if the Confederates could find a way to seriously test Point Lookout.

And that was precisely what they intended to do.

24 Beitzel, *Point Lookout Prison Camp for Confederates*, 54.

Chapter 2

JUBAL EARLY TO THE VALLEY

LIEUTENANT GENERAL Jubal A. Early played a major role in the course of the war during the summer of 1864.

The West Point-trained general had advanced through the ranks of the Army of Northern Virginia from brigade command to division leadership, and then to command of the Second Corps when Lt. Gen. Richard Ewell was no longer capable of field service. Now, he was about to become an army commander.

Early was born on November 3, 1816, near Rocky Mount in Franklin County, Virginia. He graduated eighteenth out of forty-nine in the West Point class of 1837. He served in the artillery during the Seminole wars, after which he resigned his commission to study law. He was admitted to the Virginia bar in 1840 and was soon elected to the Virginia legislature in 1841. He served but a single term before becoming the Commonwealth's Attorney for Franklin County. He would hold the position until 1852, with his tenure interrupted by service in the Mexican War. Early was a delegate to the Virginia Secession Convention in 1861 and he voted against the Ordinance of Secession. Despite opposing secession, he offered his services to Virginia governor John Letcher on May 1, 1861, and was commissioned a colonel of Virginia State

JUBAL A. EARLY

The lieutenant general and head of the Army of the Valley led the strike on Washington, D.C. during the summer of 1864 and played a role in the cavalry raid to free the prisoners at Point Lookout.

Library of Congress

Troops. He assumed command of the 24th Virginia Infantry at Lynchburg.[1]

Early went on to compile one of the finest combat records in the Army of Northern Virginia, and a well-deserved reputation as one of the great characters of the war. He stood nearly six feet tall and weighed about 170 pounds, but he appeared much older than his years because of a pronounced stoop caused by severe arthritis. His constant pain probably contributed to what a staff officer called a "snarling, raspy disposition." His "wit was quick," however, and "his satire biting, his expressions vigorous, and he was interestingly lurid and picturesque." General Robert E. Lee fondly called Early "my bad old man." A promotion to lieutenant general was his on May 31, 1864, and he formally assumed command of the Second Corps, replacing Ewell.[2]

While the Virginia army was pinned down around Richmond and Petersburg, a Union army under Maj. Gen. David "Black Dave" Hunter burned the Virginia Military Institute and Governor John Letcher's house in Lexington and took control of the upper Shenandoah Valley. Hunter and his victorious army were headed for Lynchburg. Lee knew he had to stop Hunter and find a way to seize the initiative. He instructed Early to take his Second Corps, ride the rails west, and save Lynchburg and regain possession of the Valley. If circumstances permitted, Early was to create

1 Early's 1837 West Point class included a host of future Civil War generals including Braxton Bragg, William H. French, Joseph Hooker, John Sedgwick, John C. Pemberton, Arnold Elzey, and William H. T. Walker. This especially notable class included three Confederate army commanders and a commander of the Army of the Potomac.

2 Gary W. Gallagher, "Jubal Anderson Early," in William C. Davis and Julie Hoffman, eds., *The Confederate General*, 6 vols. (New York: National Historical Society, 1991), 2:89-90. For a full-length biography of Early, see Benjamin Franklin Cooling, III, *Jubal Early: Robert E. Lee's Bad Old Man* (New York: Rowman & Littlefield, 2014).

DAVID HUNTER

A major general, "Black Dave" Hunter defeated by Early at Lynchburg and left the route to the Potomac River undefended.

Library of Congress

havoc there and menace the Federal capital at Washington, D.C., disrupt the Baltimore & Ohio Railroad (the "B&O"), the most important Union supply line, and disrupt Northern communications.[3]

Lee hoped to replay the events of 1862. That second spring of the war, Maj. Gen. Thomas J. "Stonewall" Jackson's small Valley army had caused sufficient chaos in the same theater to force Maj. Gen. George B. McClellan to send troops to the Valley and away from his own operation. Lee hoped that if Early could menace the Northern capital, Lt. Gen. Ulysses S. Grant, who was in command of all Union forces, would have no choice but to do the same thing, i.e., detach troops from the front lines at Richmond and Petersburg to save Washington. If he could be forced to do so, Lee would have a better chance of breaking the Union army's death grip. Lee may also have hoped that Early's activities might impact the 1864 presidential election in the North late that fall.

After extraordinarily hard and bloody service during the Overland Campaign, the Second Corps "numbered a little over 8,000 muskets for duty," Early reported. His new command, he continued,

> had been on active and arduous service in the field for forty days and had been engaged in all of the great battles from the Wilderness to Cold Harbor, sustaining very heavy losses at Spotsylvania Court House, where it lost nearly an entire division, including its commander, Major General [Edward] Johnson, who was made prisoner.
>
> Constant exposure to the weather, a limited supply of provisions, and two weeks' service in the swamps north of the Chickahominy had told on the health of the men. Divisions were not stronger than brigades ought to have been, nor brigades than regiments.[4]

3 *OR* 37, 1:346.

4 Jubal A. Early, *Autobiographical Sketch and Narrative of the War Between the States* (Philadelphia: J. B. Lippincott, 1912), 371-372.

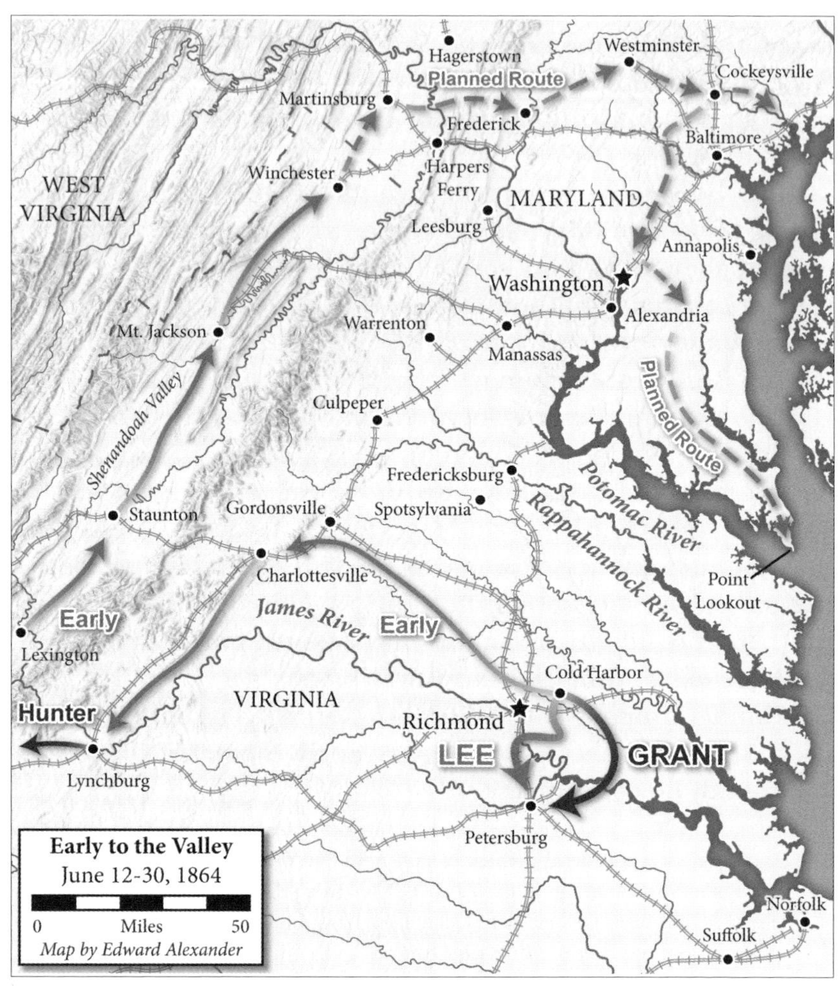

Early to the Valley
June 12-30, 1864
0 Miles 50
Map by Edward Alexander

If Early was to have any hope of success, however, he would need reinforcements for his mission. The division of Maj. Gen. John C. Breckinridge and some miscellaneous cavalry forces from the Valley District joined the Second Corps, and the little command was soon dubbed the Army of the Valley.

The Southerners marched from the stagnant battle lines at Cold Harbor on June 12. Upon reaching Charlottesville,

Early's troops boarded trains of the Virginia Central Railroad that carried them to Lynchburg, where they arrived on June 18 just in time to meet Hunter's advance. In two days of fighting on June 18 and 19, Early drove Hunter away from Lynchburg and back into West Virginia.[5]

Hunter failed to advise Grant that he had been routed, so the Union high command was unable to take steps to guard the Shenandoah Valley routes leading north to the Potomac River. Hunter was effectively out of the war for almost a month, meaning that there were no Union forces of any significance remaining in the Valley to prevent Early from marching quickly north and threatening Washington. The route to the Potomac River was clear.[6]

On June 23, Early wired Lee to tell him that Hunter had retreated into West Virginia. This move, he added, would allow Early to proceed with his original instructions, which were to secure the Shenandoah Valley, cross into Maryland, and attack Washington, if possible.[7]

"I deemed it best to turn down the Valley and proceed according to your instructions, to threaten Washington and if I find an opportunity to take it," he penned Lee three days later. Early advised Lee that only a small force of 100 days' emergency troops remained in the lower (northern) Shenandoah Valley, meaning that the way to the Potomac River was unobstructed. Early asked that Bradley Johnson

5 Ibid., 160. For a detailed discussion of the fighting between Early and Hunter at Lynchburg, see Scott C. Patchan, *The Battle of Piedmont and Hunter's Raid on Staunton: The 1864 Shenandoah Campaign* (Charleston, SC: The History Press, 2011).

6 This is not intended to be an exhaustive account of Early's strike down (meaning north) the Shenandoah Valley and raid into Maryland. For a solid account of the campaign, see Benjamin Franklin Cooling, III, *Jubal Early's Raid on Washington 1864* (Mt. Pleasant, SC: Nautical & Aviation Publishing Co., 1989).

7 Early, *Autobiographical Sketch*, 380.

ROBERT E. LEE

The commander of the Army of Northern Virginia and the architect of the raid on Lookout Point.

Library of Congress

be promoted to brigadier general and indicated that he wanted Johnson's cavalry to destroy the bridges of the Baltimore & Ohio Railroad to deprive the enemy its benefits.[8]

On June 26, Lee advised President Jefferson Davis that Hunter had escaped and remained a threat, but that Early should be allowed to proceed with the plan as devised. The Virginia army commander believed Early should advance north down the Valley in the hope of inducing Hunter to pursue him. If circumstances permitted, Early should cross the Potomac while Lee held the Army of the Potomac in place at Petersburg and Richmond. Lee, as he often did, allowed his detached general wide discretion. Early would be the one to determine whether he could execute the plan as conceived. Early soon replied to Lee that he intended to carry out the plan.[9]

* * *

Bradley T. Johnson and his brigade of Virginia and Maryland cavalrymen reinforced Early on June 23, the same day Early and his 16,000-man Army of the Valley marched from Lynchburg. This brigade consisted primarily of men from southwestern Virginia and numbered about 1,500 men "fairly mounted, but most indifferently armed and equipped," recalled Johnson's adjutant George W. Booth. "The principal arm was the long musket, which was terribly unwieldy on horseback. There was good material in the ranks and some

8 Jubal A. Early to Robert E. Lee, June 28, 1864, CW 100 Collection, Archives, Huntington Library, San Marino, California.

9 Linda Laswell Crist, ed., *The Papers of Jefferson Davis*, 14 vols. (Baton Rouge: Louisiana State University Press, 1999), 10:484; Early *Autobiographical Sketch*, 380.

few officers of decided merit and ability." They were an undisciplined lot, but they were also hard fighters.[10]

Three days after leaving Lynchburg the Valley army reached Staunton. Four days later, on June 30, Early's command had covered the nearly fifty miles to Lexington, and by July 2 occupied Winchester. Lee instructed Early to remain in the lower Shenandoah Valley "until everything was in readiness to cross the Potomac." Lee wanted the Baltimore & Ohio to be cut west from Harpers Ferry into West Virginia.[11]

The Army of the Valley covered another forty miles in two days and reached the Potomac River crossings at Williamsport, Maryland, on July 4. Echoing the glory days of Jackson's "foot cavalry," the Valley army had covered nearly 220 miles in just eleven days, marching all the way to the Potomac River without meeting significant opposition. The road to Washington did indeed appear to be unobstructed.

Between Winchester and Martinsburg, Early divided his forces. He directed General Johnson's cavalry brigade and a brigade of infantry in Maj. Gen. Stephen D. Ramseur's Division to move to the right under Early's personal command to cut the Baltimore & Ohio at Kearneysville and thereafter unite with Brig. Gen. John McCausland's cavalry and John C. Breckinridge's infantry at Martinsburg. Once that happened, Johnson and McCausland would coalesce at Hainesville, five miles northeast of Martinsburg on the Valley Turnpike, and cut off the retreat route of Maj. Gen. Franz Sigel's Union command from Martinsburg. Sigel and his entire force, however, managed to escape to Harpers Ferry and hole up on Maryland Heights. The balance of Early's

10 George W. Booth, *Personal Reminiscences of a Maryland Soldier in the War Between the States, 1861-1865* (Baltimore: Fleet, McGinley & Co., 1898), 122-123; Early, *Autobiographical Sketch*, 380-382.

11 Ibid., 382-383.Early, *Autobiographical Sketch*, 382-383.

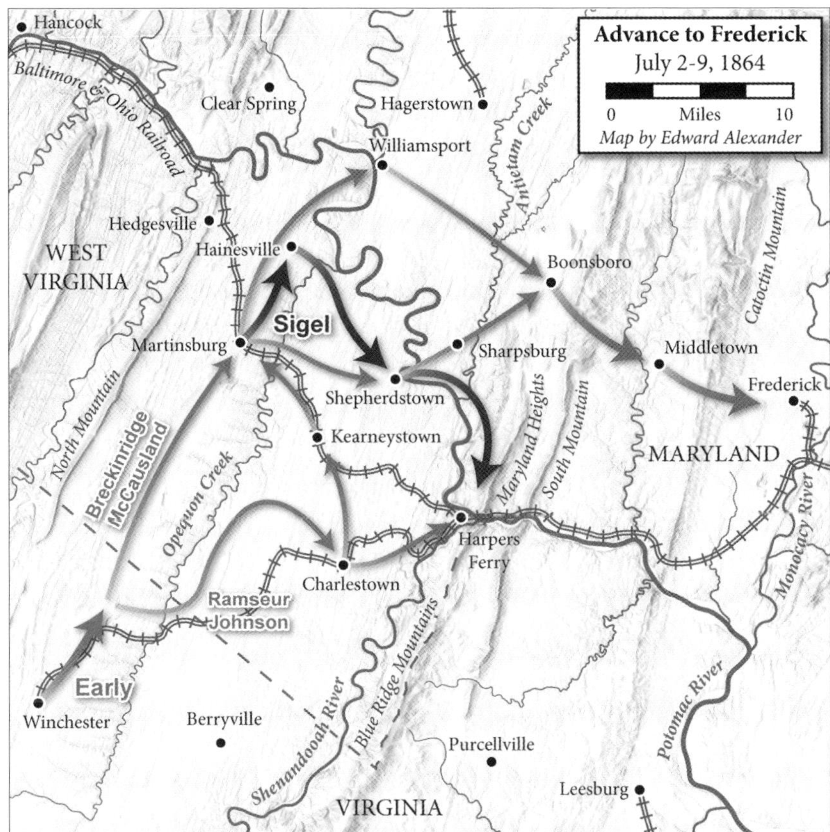

army, meanwhile, continued marching toward the Potomac River crossings at Williamsport and Shepherdstown.[12]

By the night of July 5 Johnson's cavalry, which constituted the advance elements of Early's army, established camp near Boonsboro. The next day Johnson rode his troopers to Middletown, and on the 7th skirmished with a small force of the 8th Illinois Cavalry on South Mountain between Middletown and Frederick. The Rebels

12 *OR* 37, 1:347; Bradley T. Johnson, "My Ride Around Baltimore in Eighteen Hundred and Sixty-Four," *SHSP*, 30:217.

drove the Union troopers back to the latter town, securing the critical South Mountain passes for use by Early's army.

Johnson was born and raised in the Frederick area so he knew every inch of its ground. The cavalry general insisted on sending a force into Frederick to capture the Union garrison there, but his commanding officer, Maj. Gen. Robert Ransom, Jr., refused to give Johnson permission. Instead, Ransom ordered Johnson to withdraw under the cover of night to the top of the range and await the arrival of the infantry.[13]

* * *

The Union high command was well aware of the threat posed to Washington by Early's army, and much of its knowledge came from John W. Garrett. The 43-year old Baltimore native and the son of an Irish immigrant attended college for a time before working as a clerk and apprentice in his father's mercantile, banking, and financial services firm. He learned the business from the bottom up. The company's operations expanded west with the opening of the National Road toward the Mississippi River and would eventually reach California and the southwest. Garrett and his brother

13 Ransom was an experienced infantry officer with a decidedly mixed record of field success. Robert E. Lee had transferred him and his division to his home state in January of 1863. He was promoted to major general on May 26, 1863 and defended the critical Weldon Railroad and a section of southeastern Virginia. By May 1864 he had returned to southeastern Virginia and assumed command of a four-brigade division, which fell apart, at least in part due to Ransom's poor performance, during an attack at Drewry's Bluff on May 16. He was transferred to command of the cavalry in the Valley District in June 1864 to command the cavalry units assigned to Early's army. Ransom took leave due to health problems in the fall of 1864 and retired from service. Ransom's brother Matthew was also a Confederate general. Jeffry D. Wert, "Robert Ransom, Jr.," in William C. Davis and Julie Hoffman, eds., *The Confederate General*, 6 vols. (New York: National Historical Society, 1991), 5:80-81.

JOHN W. GARRETT

The president of the Baltimore & Ohio Railroad played a major role in defending Washington from Jubal Early's army.

B & O Railroad Museum

Henry took over the company's operations, and when Henry joined the board of directors of the B&O in 1847, John followed suit. In 1858, at the behest of board member Johns Hopkins (namesake of the eponymous Baltimore university) Garrett became the rail line's new president, a position he would hold until the 1880s.[14]

Garrett's role with such a vital logistical artery put him in close contact with people in high places—including President Lincoln. Confederate Vice President Alexander Stevens would later claim the Confederacy had been doomed from "the early months, after the fall of Fort Sumter, when the South was waiting for Maryland to act and Lincoln prevented that state from seceding—largely because of the overwhelming influence exerted by the Baltimore & Ohio in favor of the Washington government." Indeed, at the end of the Civil War Lincoln described Garrett as "The right arm of the Federal Government in the aid he rendered the authorities in preventing the Confederates from seizing Washington and securing its retention as the Capital of the Loyal States."[15]

An early West Virginia historian agreed that Garrett had such influence when he recorded that the railroad president "was as much a part of Mr. Lincoln's Cabinet as any man in it, and was often called to Cabinet councils when questions of grave moment were to be discussed." One such "grave moment" was the approach of Early's Valley army during the summer of 1864.[16]

The president of the B&O worked slavishly to keep the telegraph lines humming with frequent detailed and accurate intelligence reports as the veteran Southern force bore down

14 Kathleen Waters Sander, *John W. Garrett and the Baltimore & Ohio Railroad* (Baltimore, MD: Johns Hopkins University Press, 2017), 71-78.

15 Ibid., 173.

16 Theodore F. Lang, *Loyal West Virginia From 1861 to 1865* (Baltimore, MD: The Deutsch Publishing Co., 1895),146.

on his railroad during its march toward the Potomac. By July 5 there was no doubt about the threat posed by the approaching enemy.[17]

But how great was the threat? There was no doubt a small Rebel army was heading north, but surely General Hunter's army could handle it? General Grant was still under the mistaken impression that Hunter could defend the national capital, not yet grasping that the general had withdrawn his army into West Virginia and cleared the way north for Early. As a result, Grant ordered a single division of the VI Corps under Brig. Gen. James Ricketts, together with all of the dismounted cavalry troopers of the Army of the Potomac's Second Cavalry Division, to report to Washington to reinforce the understrength garrison manning the capital's defenses.[18]

Because Hunter's army was nowhere to be seen, the primary defense of the crucial B&O and Baltimore and Washington fell upon the 7,000 soldiers of the VIII Corps commanded by Maj. Gen. Lew Wallace. Because of their past history, Grant and Wallace did not much like one another.

Lewis Wallace was born in Brookville, Indiana, on April 10, 1827, but moved to Indianapolis while still young when his father was elected governor of Indiana. The precocious youth pursued a number of fields including clerical duties, politics, history, and the law. After serving his country as a first lieutenant of the 1st Indiana during the Mexican War, he was admitted to the bar a few years later and elected to the state senate in 1856.

17 Among his many contributions, Garrett organized and executed the funeral train that carried the body of the assassinated Abraham Lincoln home to Springfield, Illinois, for burial. Sander, *John W. Garrett and the Baltimore & Ohio Railroad*, 169-170.

18 *OR* 37, 2:60. Grant told Maj. Gen. George G. Meade, the commander of the Army of the Potomac, "I will not send an army corps until there is greater necessity for it." Ibid.

His connected position made it possible for Governor Oliver P. Morton to appoint him state adjutant general during the first April of the war. That wasn't enough to satisfy Wallace's ardor for the field, and soon thereafter he was commissioned colonel of the 11th Indiana, a three-month regiment that reenlisted for three years.

Service in western Virginia followed, as did a promotion to brigadier general on September 3. His course was firmly set when he was shipped west and took part in the capture of Fort Donelson in February 1862—his first service under U. S. Grant. Another promotion arrived, this one to major general of volunteers to rank from March 21, 1862. It was then that everything changed.

Less than three weeks later during the early stages of the fighting at Shiloh, Grant instructed Wallace to march his division upstream from Crump's Landing on the Tennessee River to the battlefield. Wallace lost his way, made a lengthy countermarch, and arrived too late to deliver the crushing blow Grant hoped his division would provide. Grant won the battle in decisive fashion, but relieved Wallace of command and exiled him to backwater commands for the next two years. War offers up odd strokes of fortune, good and ill.[19]

Fortunately for Grant and the Union, these days of crisis in 1864 would prove to be Wallace's finest hour. With no other blocking force upon which he could count, the Indianan set about preparing a defense of the critical railroad junction just south of Frederick, Maryland, at a place called Monocacy Junction.

19 Warner, *Generals in Blue*, 535-56. After the Civil War Wallace became internationally famous as the author of the novel *Ben Hur: A Tale of the Christ*. For a full-length biography of Wallace, see Gail Stephens, *Shadow of Shiloh: Major General Lew Wallace in the Civil War* (Indianapolis: Indiana Historical Society, 2010).

Chapter 3

General Lee's Audacious Plan to Free the Prisoners at Point Lookout

DURING THE winter of 1863-1864, Bradley T. Johnson, at that time a colonel, developed a bold plan to capture President Abraham Lincoln.

Confederate spies in Washington, D.C. kept Gen. Robert E. Lee apprised of events within the Union capital. It was well-known that Lincoln spent summers not at the White House but at the Soldiers Home in the northeastern quadrant of the city. Johnson proposed to take the Maryland Cavalry Battalion—approximately 250 sabers—across the Potomac above Georgetown, attack the detachment of the 2nd Massachusetts Cavalry stationed there, push on to the Soldiers Home, and capture Lincoln.[1]

Once the chief executive was in Johnson's hands, the cavalryman would send the president across the Potomac with a small detachment while the main body cut telegraph wires and wrecked railroads between Baltimore and

1 Johnson, "My Ride Around Baltimore," 215.

Washington. When the time was right, the entire force would escape into Virginia via western Maryland or, if that route was blocked, ride north into Pennsylvania and cross into West Virginia near Grafton. "It seemed, indeed, a desperate undertaking, but everything promised its successful accomplishment," noted a Marylander. General Lee learned of Johnson's plan and began developing his own thoughts about it. Lee contemplated originating the operation from Hanover Court House north of Richmond.[2]

In early February of 1864, Union Brig. Gen. Isaac J. Wistar, based near Yorktown on the Virginia Peninsula, prepared to lead a raid of his own intended to free Union prisoners being held in Richmond's infamous Libby Prison and on Belle Isle (in the James River), capture Confederate public officials, and destroy public property and stores. The scheme was the brainchild of Wistar's commander, Maj. Gen. Benjamin F. Butler. The raid never took place. It was called off when a Union deserter told the Confederates about it. The canceled plan, however, made it clear that the Northern high command was interested in finding a way to free prisoners held in Richmond at Belle Isle and Libby Prison.[3]

It was not long thereafter that they tried once again. On February 28 a force of about 4,000 Union cavalrymen in two columns commanded by Brig. Gen. Judson Kilpatrick and Col. Ulric Dahlgren departed from the Army of the Potomac's winter encampment in Culpeper County, Virginia. While Kilpatrick and about 3,500 troopers demonstrated around

2 Johnson, "My Ride Around Baltimore," 216; William W. Goldsborough, *The Maryland Line in the Confederate Army, 1861-1865* (Baltimore: Guggenheimer, Weil, and Co., 1900), 203.

3 Goldsborough, *The Maryland Line in the Confederate Army*, 244; Benjamin F. Butler, *Private and Personal Correspondence of Gen. Benjamin F. Butler During the Period of the Civil War*, 5 vols. (Norwood, MA: Plimpton Press, 1917), 3:373-374.

the northern defenses of Richmond, 500 selected troopers under Dahlgren would dash into Richmond and free the prisoners.

Dahlgren and his troopers failed to force their way through the defenses of Richmond and were repulsed. Kilpatrick lost his nerve and retreated after Maj. Gen. Wade Hampton's cavalry division attacked him near Atlee's Station on the Virginia Central Railroad north of the Southern capital. Young Dahlgren was killed trying to lead his command to safety, and papers found on his body suggested that the raid not only intended to free the prisoners, but kidnap and assassinate Confederate President Jefferson Davis and his cabinet and burn Richmond. As was to be expected, Maj. Gen. George G. Meade, the commander of the Army of the Potomac, disavowed Dahlgren. And there the matter ended.

Confederate authorities, however, remained as outraged about the failed effort as they were worried about further attempts to free the prisoners. Belle Isle and Libby Prison were shut down, and the captives put aboard trains and sent south. Many ended up in a much worse place: a new prisoner of war pen in Georgia called Camp Sumter, better known as Andersonville.[4]

The audacious failure that was the Kilpatrick-Dahlgren Raid convinced General Lee to postpone his plan to send Johnson off to try and kidnap President Lincoln. A frustrated Johnson clung to his idea and engaged in numerous discussions with his cavalry division commander, Wade Hampton, about how to bring the plan to fruition. The persuasive subordinate eventually convinced his superior of its merits. "Indeed, so sanguine was Hampton that Johnson's

4 For a detailed study of the failed Kilpatrick-Dahlgren Raid, see Bruce M. Venter, *Kill Jeff Davis: The Union Raid on Richmond, 1864* (Norman: University of Oklahoma Press, 2016).

JEFFERSON DAVIS

The Confederate president approved the attempt to free the prisoners of war held at Point Lookout.

Library of Congress

plan would succeed that he wanted to undertake it himself at the head of four thousand horse," reported Rebel Maryland officer William Goldsborough. Hampton was "only prevented from doing so by [Philip H.] Sheridan's advance on the Confederate Capital" in May 1864.[5]

After defeating Sheridan's cavalry at Trevilian Station on June 11-12, Hampton finally gave Johnson permission to attempt his daring scheme. After choosing the best soldiers in his command the Marylander made sure the healthiest horses were also selected and shod in preparation to make the exhausting expedition. An unexpected interruption arrived in the form of orders from Jubal Early directing Johnson and his Maryland horsemen to report to him near Lynchburg, Virginia. Johnson's promotion to brigadier general also came through at that time. The elevation in rank allowed him to assume command of a brigade of Virginia cavalry formerly commanded by Brig. Gen. William E. Jones, who had been killed at the Battle of Piedmont on June 5, 1864. The Virginia cavalry joined Johnson's new brigade, swelling its numbers to about 1,500 troopers.[6]

Johnson reported as directed, and did not waste any time before telling the infantry general about his plan. Early waved off the idea. "I'm going to Lynchburg," he declared, "and as soon as I smash up Mr. Hunter's little tea party, I'm going to Washington myself. You'll put all that out, so you musn't try it until I come back." Johnson, continued Early, was to move to Staunton and watch the Shenandoah Valley until he got there. Johnson's plan to try to kidnap Lincoln was scrubbed. What Johnson had yet to learn was that a more audacious plan would soon replace it.[7]

5 Goldsborough, *The Maryland Line*, 203.

6 Ibid.

7 Johnson, "My Ride Around Baltimore," 216.

* * *

On June 26, 1864, General Lee penned a long letter to President Davis. After stating that Hunter had escaped Early and will "make good his retreat," Lee discussed the strategic situation and the likelihood he would have to attack Grant directly outside Petersburg and recall Early from the Valley. It was then that Lee turned to the matter of the proposed raid on Point Lookout. "I should like much to have the benefit of your Excellency's good judgment, and views upon the subject," he began. "Great benefit might be drawn from the release of our prisoners from Point Lookout if it can be accomplished." The remarkable communication is worth quoting at length. Lee continued:

> The number of men employed for this purpose would necessarily be small, as the whole would have to be transported secretly across the Potomac where it is very broad, the means of doing which must first be procured. I can devote to this purpose the whole of the Marylanders of this army, which would afford a sufficient number of men of excellent material, and much experience but I am at a loss where to find a proper leader. As he would command Maryland troops and operate upon Maryland soil, it would be well that he should be a Marylander. Of those connected with this army, I consider Col. Bradley Johnson, the most suitable, he is bold & intelligent, ardent & true, and yet I am unable to say, whether he possesses all the requisite qualities. Everything in an expedition of the kind would depend upon the leader. I have understood that most of the garrison at Pt. Lookout was composed of negroes. I should suppose that the commander of such troops would be poor & feeble. A stubborn resistance therefore may reasonably not be expected. By taking a company of the Md. artillery, armed as infantry, the dismounted cavalry and their infantry organization, as many men would be supplied as transportation could be procured for. By throwing them suddenly on the beach with some concert of action among the prisoners, I think the guard might be overpowered, the prisoners liberated & organized, and marched immediately on the route to Washington.

Lee continued:

> The artillery command could operate the guns captured at the Point. The dismounted cavalry with the released prisoners of that army, could mount themselves on the march, and the infantry would form a respectable force. Such a body of men under an able leader although they will not be able without assistance to capture Washington, could march around it, and cross the upper Potomac where fordable. I do not think they could cross the river in a body at any point below Washington, unless possibly at Alexandria. Provisions &c., would have to be collected in the country through which they pass. The operations on the river must be confided to an able Naval officer, who I know will be found in Col. [John Taylor] Wood. The subject is one worthy of consideration and can only be matured by reflection.
>
> The sooner it is put in execution, the better, if it be deemed practicable.[8]

Although the plan smacked, at best, of rank desperation, the operation offered General Lee the chance to reinforce his depleted army and threaten the Federal capital at Washington at the same time.

General Early wrote to Lee from Staunton two days later on June 28 to keep him apprised of his plans. "When I am in Maryland I will send a select body of cavalry to cut the railroads between Washington and Harrisburg and Baltimore and Philadelphia while I am moving on Washington," explained the Valley army leader. "I shall make every effort to release our prisoners at Point Lookout. How much of this I may be able to accomplish will depend on circumstances, but no effort of mine will be spared to accomplish all, and I hope

8 Lee to Davis, June 26, 1864, included in Laswell, *The Papers of Jefferson Davis*, 10:485. No reply from Davis has been located.

at least to obtain some relief for you from the purpose brought against you."[9]

Lee wrote to Davis once again On June 29. "I think it is our policy to draw the attention of the enemy to his own territory," he advocated. "It may force Grant to attack me or weaken himself to attack. From either of these events, I anticipate good results; news of Johnson's success will help Early; liberation of Point Lookout would also be useful."[10]

* * *

Brigadier General Bradley T. Johnson remains little-known among students of the Civil War, but he was a fine choice to command the daring expedition.

He was born in Frederick, Maryland, on September 29, 1829 and graduated from Princeton University two decades later. During the years leading up to the war he became a prominent state's attorney, a respected orator, and the chairman of the Maryland Democratic Party. Johnson backed John C. Breckinridge for president in 1860, and when actual fighting broke out decided to support the Confederate cause.

John Letcher, Virginia's governor, offered Johnson a commission as a lieutenant colonel but he declined in order help organize Maryland units for the Confederacy. He helped recruit and organize the 1st Maryland Infantry and that June was commissioned a major in the new regiment. When its two senior officers (Arnold Elzey and George H. Steuart) fell wounded at Manassas, Johnson assumed command of the regiment. The promotion of Elzey to brigadier general and Steuart to colonel bumped Johnson to lieutenant colonel of

9 Early to Lee, June 28, 1864.

10 Crist, *The Papers of Jefferson Davis*, 10:493.

BRADLEY T. JOHNSON

The Maryland native who designed a plan to kidnap President Abraham Lincoln would lead a cavalry brigade in a daring raid to free Rebel prisoners.

Library of Congress

the regiment, and in the spring of 1862, when Steuart was promoted to brigadier, Johnson was elevated to colonel and found himself in command of the 1st Maryland.

Johnson's first true test as a leader arrived during Thomas J. "Stonewall" Jackson's Valley Campaign in the spring of 1862. The term of one of the 12-month companies in the 1st Maryland expired on May 17, and its members pressed to be released from service. George Steuart was a brigadier organizing the Maryland Line and no longer in command, leaving Johnson as the regiment's colonel to deal with the thorny matter. Johnson understood their concerns and the terms of their enlistment, but Jackson's small army was in the middle of an active campaign. Nothing could be done at the moment.[11]

The anger felt by the men erupted into what can only be described as open mutiny by May 22 just before the Battle of Front Royal. Both Steuart and Johnson pleaded and argued with the troops without result, making sure all the while to keep the matter as quiet as possible and away from the eyes and ears of Stonewall Jackson. With battle about to be joined and orders circulating, Johnson personally addressed his recalcitrant soldiers.

"You have heard the order, and I must confess are in a pretty condition to obey it," declared the colonel. "I will have to return it with the endorsement upon the back that 'the First Maryland refuses to meet the enemy" even though directed to do so by Jackson himself. He continued:

> Before this day I was proud to call myself a Marylander, but now, God knows, I would rather be known as anything else. Shame on you to bring this stigma upon the fair name of your native state—to cause the finger of scorn to be pointed at those who confided to your keeping their most sacred trust—their honor and that of the glorious Old State.

11 Goldsborough, *The Maryland Line in the Confederate Army*, 45.

Marylanders you call yourselves," he added. "[P]rofane not that hallowed name again, for it is not yours."[12]

According to one of his officers, Johnson was only getting started. "What Marylander," he continued,

> ever before threw down his arms and deserted his colors in the presence of the enemy, and those arms, and those colors too, placed in your hands by a woman? Never before has one single blot defaced her honored history. Could it be possible to conceive a crime more atrocious, an outrage more damnable? Go home and publish to the world your infamy. Boast of it when you meet your fathers and mothers, brothers, sisters and sweethearts. Tell them it was you who, when brought face to face with the enemy, proved yourselves recreants, and acknowledged yourselves to be cowards. Tell them this, and see if you are not spurned from their presence like some loathsome leper, and despised, detested, nay abhorred, by those whose confidence you have so shamefully betrayed; you will wander over the face of the earth with the brand of 'coward', 'traitor,' indelibly imprinted on your foreheads, and in the end sink into a dishonored grave, unwept for, uncared for, leaving behind as a heritage to your posterity the scorn and contempt of every honest man and virtuous woman in the land.

Johnson's bold dressing-down struck a nerve with these proud men, who rallied to battle crying, "lead us to the enemy and we will prove to you that we are not cowards."[13]

There was still much fighting to do. On May 25 Johnson and his 1st Maryland fought in what would be the first of three battles at Winchester; two weeks later they fought again

12 Goldsborough, *The Maryland Line*, 49.

13 Ibid. The fighting at Front Royal on May 23, 1862, pitted the Confederate 1st Maryland against fellow Marylanders fighting with 1st Regiment Maryland Volunteer Infantry. This was the first time in American history that two regiments with the same numerical designation from the same state engaged one another in battle.

at Cross Keys on June 8, where Johnson helped direct a stout defensive effort.

William Goldsborough, whose fascinating and well-written postwar memoir sheds significant light on the role of Johnson and the Marylanders in camp and on the battlefield, described the regimental colonel as "one of the handsomest men in the First Maryland." On at least one occasion, so goes the unique telling by Goldsborough, Johnson's good looks attracted female attention:

> having dismounted from his horse in an unguarded moment, [he] was espied and singled out by an old lady of Amazonian proportions, just from the wash tub, who, wiping her hands and mouth on her apron as she approached, seized him around the neck with the hug of a bruin, and bestowed upon him half a dozen kisses that were heard by nearly every man in the command, and when at length she relaxed her hold the Colonel looked as if he had just come out a vapor bath.[14]

Johnson's regiment accompanied Jackson's command in the move east to join the main army around Richmond, where the Marylanders fought during the Seven Days' Battles. When the 1st Maryland disbanded that August Johnson may have served for a time unofficially on Jackson's staff. After Cedar Mountain he temporarily succeeded to the command of the wounded Brig. Gen. John R. Jones's former Virginia brigade (then operating under Col. Thomas Garnett) and led it well at Second Manassas.

Johnson would have known his assignment was a stopgap measure, but he could not have known that he would never lead another infantry brigade during the rest of the war. The border state native was the victim of the ultra-sensitive state pride that ruled Confederate assignments and promotions to an immense degree. Johnson was from

14 Ibid., 59.

Maryland, there were but few Maryland organizations in Southern service, and never remotely enough for a brigade.[15]

As a result, the Army of Northern Virginia moved north into Maryland early that September with a captain at the head of the Virginia brigade Johnson had so briefly commanded. With no suitable command the Marylander assumed provost marshal duties and missed the heavy fighting at Sharpsburg.[16]

The middle of the war was a low point for Johnson. He spent months in administrative positions and on a military court in Richmond, and in so doing missed Fredericksburg, Chancellorsville, Gettysburg, and the Fall 1863 campaigns. He assumed temporary command of the Maryland Line Cavalry—the 1st Maryland Cavalry and the Baltimore Light Artillery—in the fall of 1863. It was not until after the death of Brig. Gen. William E. Jones on June 5, 1864, that Johnson was finally promoted to brigadier general—after having been recommended for promotion by Stonewall Jackson twice. With his stars and collar wreath Johnson assumed command of Jones's mounted brigade, which now included the 1st and 2nd Maryland Cavalry.[17]

And so it was that Johnson now found himself a brigadier at the head of a cavalry command with Jubal Early's Valley army in its move north of the Potomac. Having been raised in the Frederick area, he knew that part of Maryland like the back of his hand. Because of his prewar activities he was

15 Email from Robert K. Krick, July 10, 2022. For more details and sources on Johnson, see Lydia Habliston Davis, "Bradley T. Johnson, Brigadier General, C.S.A.," Master's Thesis, Virginia Polytechnic and State University, 1973.

16 John E. Olson, "Bradley T. Johnson," in Richard N. Current, ed., *The Encyclopedia of the Confederacy*, 4 vols. (Simon & Schuster, 1993), 2: 849.

17 See Jeffry D. Wert, "Bradley Tyler Johnson," in Davis and Hoffman, eds., *The Confederate General*, 3:172-179.

well-known throughout the region, and within the army he had the respect of the soldiers. If anyone could lead this sort of a daring and dangerous expedition successfully, it was Johnson.

* * *

General Lee had also suggested to President Davis that the effort to free the prisoners at Point Lookout consist of a combined-arms operation. "The operations on the river must be confided to an able Naval officer, who I know will be found in Col. [John Taylor] Wood," suggested the general.[18]

Wood had an interesting background. He was born at Fort Snelling, Iowa Territory (now St. Paul, Minnesota) on August 13, 1830. His father Robert Crooke Wood was a U.S. Army surgeon and his mother Anna Mackall Taylor, was the eldest daughter of General (later U.S. President) Zachary Taylor. Anna's youngest sister was Jefferson Davis's first wife, meaning that Davis was Wood's uncle by marriage. Wood's father eventually achieved the rank of brevet major general in the United States Army.

John Wood applied in 1847 for admission to the U.S. Naval Academy at Annapolis, Maryland, and was appointed an acting midshipman that same year. So began his extensive service at sea. His first assignment was on the frigate *Brandywine* and then the U.S.S. *Ohio*. In 1849 he was warranted a midshipman and ordered back to Annapolis. In less than six months he was on the high seas once more, this time aboard the sloop of war *Germantown* in service against the African slave trade. By 1852 he was back at the Naval Academy, where he graduated in June 1853.

18 *OR* 37, 1:766-768.

JOHN TAYLOR WOOD

The adventurous captain, who also held a commission as a colonel in the Confederate army, was picked to lead the seaborne expedition to Point Lookout.

Library of Congress

Wood served in the Mediterranean Sea aboard the U.S.S. *Cumberland* (the same warship sunk by the CSS *Virginia* in Hampton Roads in early 1862) until 1855, when he returned to the Naval Academy with the rank of Acting Master and Assistant Commandant of Midshipmen. In November of that year he was promoted to Master, and one year later commissioned lieutenant. Wood went on to serve aboard the steam frigate *Wabash* until he was ordered back to the Naval

Academy in 1860 to serve as Instructor in Naval Tactics and Gunnery.

Despite his family pedigree and place of birth, young Wood cast his lot with the Confederacy when the secession crisis broke out. He resigned his naval commission in May of 1861 in exchange for a lieutenant's commission that October in the nearly nonexistent Confederate States Navy. After a tour of duty with shore batteries he was assigned to the C.S.S. *Virginia*, an ironclad being built from the ruins of the wrecked U.S.S. *Merrimack*. Wood commanded the *Virginia's* aft pivot gun and participated in the epic battle with the U.S.S. *Monitor* at Hampton Roads that March.

In October of 1862 Wood assumed command of a small squadron of wooden warships. His hit and run tactics up and down Chesapeake Bay garnered significant if minor successes that caught the attention of his superiors. The result was a promotion to commander in the Navy and a simultaneous commission as a colonel in the Confederate Army. He was serving as a liaison between the branches and also as naval aide to his uncle, President Davis, when the chance to join the operation to free the prisoners was raised with him.[19]

Wood was educated, experienced, gallant, and reliable—a fine choice to command the naval prong of the expedition.

* * *

The waterborne portion of the plan was as tricky as it was desperate because it demanded coordination with Johnson's cavalry strike. While the Marylander and his troopers

19 Charles S. Schwartz, "John Taylor Wood: Confederate Commando," *Military Images*, 2 (July-August 1980), 4-5. For a full-length biography of Wood, see Royce G. Shingleton, *John Taylor Wood: Sea Ghost of the Confederacy* (Athens: University of Georgia Press, 1979).

GEORGE WASHINGTON CUSTIS LEE

General Lee's eldest son, the proposed commander of the ground troops for the amphibious portion of the seaborne expedition, had long yearned for a command in the field.

Library of Congress

executed the lengthy ride across Maryland to attack the prison camp from the land side, a ship commanded by Wood with 800 marines and sailors under General Lee's oldest son, Brig. Gen. George Washington Custis Lee, would attack the prison camp from the water side. Wood's ship would carry with it several thousand rifled muskets to arm the freed prisoners.

The Lee tasked to lead the marines and sailors was born September 16, 1832, at Fort Monroe, Virginia. The first-born child of Robert E. and Mary Custis Lee was named for his maternal grandfather and called Custis by the family. He graduated from West Point in 1854, entered the engineers, and remained in the Regular Army until the Civil War broke out. He resigned in May of 1861 and was commissioned a captain in the Confederate Army.

Custis performed engineering duties on the Richmond fortifications and served on Jefferson Davis's staff. Ill-health plagued the younger Lee throughout the war and made it difficult for him to achieve a field command, which was something he craved. He also wanted to serve as his father's chief of staff, but the elder Lee refused. Custis was promoted to brigadier general on June 25, 1863, and continued to serve on Davis' staff. In the spring of 1864, he declined command of the District of Southwest Virginia.[20]

Now, finally, his chance to act in the field was at hand.

* * *

Coincidentally, John Taylor Wood had been independently developing his own plan to attack Point Lookout. His idea, which was much more simple and direct,

20 Jeffry D. Wert, "George Washington Custis Lee," in Davis and Hoffman, eds., *The Confederate General*, 4:42-43. Custis was promoted to major general on October 20, 1864, and during the war's final months organized the clerks and mechanics of Richmond for the capital's defenses. He was captured at Sayler's Creek on April 6, 1865, and paroled due to his mother's illness. After the war Lee accepted a professorship at Washington College in Lexington, Virginia, where his father served as president. When Robert E. Lee died in October 1870, Custis succeeded him as president of the college, a position he held, but did not enjoy, until 1897. Custis died on February 18, 1913, and was buried in the Lee family crypt on the campus of Washington College.

was to ferry Confederate troops across the wide Potomac River and attack the prison camp. The more complex two-pronged effort was finally adopted for implementation.

On July 2, Wood delivered a letter about the operation to Robert E. Lee penned by President Davis; Lee gave his hearty approval for the complex idea. The scheme, as discussed at Lee's headquarters at Petersburg, called for Wood to run the blockade at Wilmington, North Carolina, steam north and enter the Chesapeake Bay, disrupt the telegraphic cable connecting Fortress Monroe and Cherrystone Point, and head for Point Lookout. Once in position, Wood and Custis Lee would attack the prison camp from the river side at dawn on July 12 while Johnson's troopers launched a simultaneous attack from the land side. The freed prisoners would either join General Early's attack on Washington or pass to the north of Washington and cross the Upper Potomac into Virginia. Lee wrote Davis the next day, "I think under the blessing of a merciful Providence they will be successful and result in great good." He also instructed General Early to plan to rendezvous with Wood's ships "about the 12th inst."[21]

On July 4, Wood received special orders from Davis. Major General William H. C. Whiting, the Confederate commander at Wilmington, was directed to furnish Wood with two Parrott artillery pieces to cover the amphibious landing at Point Lookout. Whiting was also instructed to cooperate with Wood in every way possible. Wood, meanwhile, was directed to execute his orders and communicate closely with the general in charge of the district in which he operated (i.e., Whiting). Davis understood how

21 Shingleton, *John Taylor Wood*, 116-117; Douglas Southall Freeman, ed., *Lee's Dispatches* (New York: G. P. Putnam's Sons, 1915), 269-271.

circumstances could change without warning and he gave Wood the discretion to modify his orders as needed.[22]

The following day Custis Lee, Wood, and Lt. Col. Fleet W. Cox of the 40th Virginia Infantry, who was familiar with the lower Potomac River, met with Thaddeus Fitzhugh, a captain in the 5th Virginia Cavalry who knew the eastern shore like the back of his hand.[23]

Soon thereafter, Wood set out for Wilmington to assemble a crew and select ships for the expedition. He found a pair of sleek fast vessels, the *Let-Her B* and the *Florie*, as well as a large number of firearms. Custis Lee advised President Davis on July 8 that these weapons included some 20,000 long arms en route to Wilmington from Columbia, South Carolina, all to arm the freed prisoners.[24]

The days were passing quickly. On July 6, General Lee had dispatched another of his sons, Capt. Robert E. Lee, Jr., to deliver an important letter to Jubal Early near Shepherdstown. Lee told his son the contents of the communication and instructed him that if there was any chance he might be captured, he was to destroy the letter and report its contents to Early verbally if the opportunity arose. "He cautioned me to keep my own counsel," recalled Captain Lee, "and to say nothing to anyone about my destination."[25]

After a brief visit with his mother and sister in Richmond, Captain Lee boarded a train for Staunton. Once there, he mounted and began riding north toward the Potomac. "Riding

22 Crist, *The Papers of Jefferson Davis*, 10:407, 502.

23 William H. Tidwell, James O. Hall and David Winfred Gaddy, *Come Retribution: The Confederate Secret Service and the Assassination of President Lincoln* (Jackson, MS: University of Mississippi Press, 1988), 147. Some writers mistakenly list this meeting with Fitzhugh Lee.

24 Crist, *The Papers of Jefferson Davis*, 10:510.

25 Robert E. Lee, Jr., *Recollections and Letters of General Robert E. Lee* (New York: Doubleday, Page & Co., 1904), 131.

night and day, [I] came up with General Early at a point in Maryland some miles beyond the old battlefield at Sharpsburg," he recalled. "I delivered the letter to him, returned to Petersburg, and reported to my father." The younger Lee was "Much gratified by the evident pleasure of the General at my diligence and at the news I had brought from Early and his men, after a night's rest and two good meals I returned to my command, never telling my comrades until long afterward what had been done to me by the commanding general."[26]

"On the 6th I received a letter from General Lee by special courier," recalled Early decades later, "informing me that, on the 12th, an effort would be made to release the prisoners at Point Lookout, and directing me to take steps to unite them with my command, if the attempt was successful." Early's postwar account confirms that he was "not informed of the manner in which the attempt would be made—General Lee stating that he was not, himself, advised of the particulars."[27]

When he received this news, Early was nearly 200 miles away from Lookout. For unknown reasons, Early did not give Johnson his orders until July 8—two days after he received word of the expedition. This gave Johnson and his troopers fewer than four full days to cover all those miles. Those two

26 Ibid.

27 Early, *Autobiographical Sketch*, 385. In 1867, Early noted he received the special courier on July 6. In 1904, R. E. Lee Jr. wrote this in *Recollections and Letters of General Robert E. Lee*: "During this summer, I had occasion, once or twice, to report to him at his headquarters, once about July 1st by his special order. . . . I reported at once, and found my father expecting me, with a bed prepared. . . . I was told to rest and sleep well, as he wanted me in the morning, and that I would need all my strength. The next morning he gave me a letter to . . . Early, who, with his command, was at that time in Maryland, threatening Washington." Lee's 1904 recollection of "about July 1," means his dates may be a little fuzzy. The date was closer to July 2 for Lee Jr.'s departure as special courier.

additional days may have increased the odds that Johnson could successfully complete his mission.

Johnson wrote about his orders after the war:

> I was directed to march at daylight of the 9th to the north of Frederick and watch Early's left until I was satisfied that he was getting on all right in the battle about to take place that day below Frederick, and then strike off across the country, cut the railroad and telegraphs north of Baltimore, sweep rapidly around the city, cut the Baltimore and Ohio railroad between Washington and Baltimore, and push on rapidly so as to strike Point Lookout on the night of 12th.
>
> Captain John Taylor Wood was to be there in an armed steamer which he was to run out of Wilmington. We were to capture the place, I was to take command of the prisoners, some ten or twelve thousand, and march them up through lower Maryland to Washington, where General Early was to wait me for me. The prisoners were to be armed and equipped from the arsenals and magazines of Washington, and thus reinforced, Early's campaign might be still further aggressive.[28]

The ambitious time-frame stunned Johnson. "I told General Early that the march laid out for me was utterly impossible for man or horse to accomplish," confessed the officer. "[I]t gave me four days not ninety-six hours, to compass near three hundred miles, not counting for the time lost in destroying bridges and railroads, but that I would do what was possible for men to do."[29]

July 9, 1864, was shaping up to be a momentous day for Jubal Early's little army, and for Johnson and his horse soldiers.

28 Johnson, "My Ride Around Baltimore in 1864," 218.

29 Ibid. The reference to 200 miles is technically correct, but does not take into account that even after capturing Point Lookout, Johnson would still need to ride through southern Maryland and on to Washington, D.C. The 300 miles reflected by Johnson is him adding the additional miles necessary after capturing Point Lookout.

Chapter 4

The Naval Expedition is Canceled

The News stunned Benjamin "The Beast" Butler. Could it be true? The major general was a powerful if not altogether popular political general from Massachusetts. By the summer of 1864 he was the commander of the Department of Virginia and North Carolina. The Point Lookout prison camp was within his area of responsibility.

On July 7 Butler forwarded potentially stunning intelligence to the War Department: "A rebel deserter reports that it is part of [Jubal] Early's plan to attack Point Lookout and release the prisoners, amusing us meanwhile at Martinsburg." Always the politician, Butler distanced himself from the report in case it was false by adding, "this is sent for what it is worth."[1]

Secretary of the Navy Gideon Welles thought the news worth quite a lot. He immediately telegraphed orders to Commander Foxhall A. Parker, in charge of the Potomac Flotilla, to "Take additional precautions relative to covering

1 *Official Records of the Union and Confederate Navies in the War of the Rebellion*, 30 vols. (Washington, DC: U. S. Government Printing Office, 1894-1927), Series I, vol. 5, 458-459 (hereafter "NOR").

BENJAMIN F. BUTLER

The eccentric major general with extensive political connections was the commander of the military district that included the facilities at Point Lookout.

Library of Congress

the camp of prisoners at Point Lookout and its approaches by your gunboats." To make sure his subordinate received and understood the message Welles added the single word "Answer." Parker replied quickly: "Telegram received and will be obeyed. I [will] send another gunboat now, making three in all."[2]

It did not take long for news of Rebel intentions to leak to the press. By July 8 the Washington correspondent of the *New York Herald* was writing about the plan and reporting that "most of the prisoners at Point Lookout have been sent to Elmira, New York, and the remainder are being transferred as rapidly as possible." None of that was true.[3]

Word of the impending raid also spread through the streets of Richmond. John B. Jones, the tireless and opinionated clerk laboring in bowels of the Confederate War Department, noted in his diary on July 9, "We have rumor today of the success of a desperate expedition from Wilmington, N.C. to Point Lookout, Maryland, [that] managed to liberate the prisoners of war (20,000) confined there and to arm them." John Tyler, the son of the former U.S. President working with the Confederate government, wrote a letter to Maj. Gen. Sterling Price in Arkansas explaining the bold plan. In the event of success, declared Tyler, "This [the raid] I regard as decidedly the most brilliant idea of the war."[4]

If Tyler and Jones and others knew this much about the operation, others did, too. A nervous President Davis informed General Lee on July 8 that the expedition was being

2 Ibid., 458.

3 "News from Washington," *New York Herald*, July 8, 1864.

4 John B. Jones, *A Rebel War Clerk's Diary at the Confederate States Capital*, 2 vols. (Philadelphia: J.B. Lippincott and Co., 1866), 2:246; Tyler letter reference: www.history.navy.mil/research/histories/ship-histories/danfs/m/minnesota-i.html, accessed July 11, 2022.

plainly spoken of on the street, and questioned whether it should proceed.[5]

* * *

As far as the participants involved knew, the longshot gambit was a go.

"Will try to get out tonight am badly off for officers, but hope for the best," Wood informed the president on July 9. He was ready to run the blockade. Davis responded the next day. "Telegram of yesterday received," he acknowledged. "The object and destination of the expedition have somehow become so generally known that I fear your operations will meet with unexpected obstacles. General R. E. Lee has communicated with you and left your action to your discretion," he continued. "I suggest calm consideration and full comparison of views with General G. W. C. [Custis] Lee, and others with whom you may choose to advise."[6]

Davis was right to be worried. So was Custis Lee. The Virginia army commander's oldest son cabled Davis on the 9th to weigh in that it was his opinion the expedition would fail.[7]

The next day Maj. Gen. William H. C. Whiting contacted Davis from Wilmington. "Sent Gen. R. E. Lee dispatch yesterday. L telegraphed he [Wood] would start tonight but gentleman from Charleston reported to me object was known there. Reported it immediately & said it was on the street," explained the frustrated commander. "Sent this to Wood—Don't know what day will decide but will inform tonight—am satisfied that nothing was known here until today when

5 Crist, *The Papers of Jefferson Davis*, 10:509.

6 Ibid. 510; *OR* 40, 3:761.

7 Crist, *The Papers of Jefferson Davis*, 10:515.

became general. Great delay caused by stopping of arms from Columbia." The flummoxed Davis was at a loss to understand how operational security had been lost so quickly. The supposedly secret expedition seemed to be the topic of conversation across large swaths of the country.[8]

As Captain Wood made his final preparations to depart on July 11, Davis knew he had a major decision to make. With operational security lost, Union warships would lay off Wilmington and at the mouth of the Chesapeake Bay to destroy or capture Wood's ships. The president informed Wood and Custis Lee that the *New York Herald* had reported the transfer of the prisoners of war, though whether they had in fact been shipped away remained unknown.

Given all that he knew, Davis reluctantly aborted the water-based arm of the mission.[9]

* * *

Although word of the seaborne arm of the operation had indeed leaked, Davis's fears proved somewhat unfounded. Operational information had not yet reached the Union naval officers serving along the Atlantic coast, and would not for another week. On July 18, an officer serving on the U.S.S. *Minnesota* warned Lincoln's War Department that Captain Wood was rumored to have left Richmond with 800 volunteers for a pending operation.[10]

The preparations closer to the scene of the proposed raid, however, proved otherwise. Commander Foxhall A. Parker of the Potomac Flotilla had advance word of the operation because of Secretary Welles's telegram, and had assigned the

8 Ibid., 512.

9 Ibid., 515.

10 Shingleton, *John Taylor Wood*, 118.

gunboats *Currituck* and *Anacostia* to patrol the waters between Point Lookout and Smith's Island. Any seaborne Confederates could not approach Camp Hoffman from that direction unnoticed.[11]

* * *

Point Lookout was ready, too. General Barnes, who was now in command there, had received a dispatch on July 2 from Col. William Hoffman advising of the potential for an imminent attack. Barnes set about fortifying the place.

The general ordered the construction of a line of works fifteen to twenty feet tall along the two necks of land connecting the Point Lookout peninsula with the mainland. One line of the fortifications would face outward to defend against the potential attack, while the other line would face inward to defend against any potential prisoner uprising. A moat fifteen feet deep would protect both lines. While noteworthy, they would have done nothing against the proposed raid because the earthworks were not completed until July 27. Their value against a potential seaborne attack on July 12, or a cavalry strike about the same time would have been next to worthless.[12]

With the amphibious arm of the operation canceled, any hope to free the prisoners at Point Lookout depended upon Bradley Johnson's cavalry.

11 *NOR* 5, 438-441.

12 Beitzell, *Point Lookout Prison Camp*, 40-41, 53-54.

Chapter 5

Bradley Johnson's Ride

GENERAL JOHNSON was an experienced leader by the summer of 1864. State pride and jealous officers and politicians, coupled with the fact that not enough men from the state of Maryland had gone South, kept him away from a permanent brigade command with the infantry. The result of this situation landed him back in the field after a nearly two-year absence, this time at the head of a motley collection of horsemen saddled with an impossible task.

The orders outlining the raid surely surprised him. Johnson understood there was little chance that he could meet the aggressive schedule established for the ride to Point Lookout. Still, orders were orders, and he was determined to try and fulfill his mission.

To maintain operational security, the newly minted brigadier general informed only three of his officers about the upcoming expedition: Asst. Adj. Gen. Capt. George W. Booth, Asst. Insp. Gen. Capt. William G. Nicholas, and Col. William E. Peters, the commander of the 21st Virginia Cavalry and the brigade's executive officer. Many years later, Johnson

LEW WALLACE
Major General, commander of the VII Corps, and the losing commander at the Battle of Monocacy.
Library of Congress

came to realize that his mission secrecy was probably a mistake. My caution, he admitted, "probably cost me time, as I made an unnecessary detour in arriving at my objective."[1]

Before noon on July 9, after heavy combat had been underway for several hours at Monocacy Junction against Wallace's Union blocking force, Jubal Early sent word that his own troops were faring just fine. Johnson, he added, should begin his raid.[2]

Early's victory over the scratch force cobbled together by Wallace along the Monocacy washed a wave of consternation over Baltimore. When word of the Confederate success reached the city, citizens gathered in the streets to discuss matters and await the latest news across the telegraph lines. A committee of city officials sent a telegram to President Lincoln begging for troops to man the city's empty defenses.

1 Johnson, "My Ride Around Baltimore," 218.

2 Bradley T. Johnson, "Riding a Raid in July, 1864," *The Leader*, December 26, 1902.

The same city officials also restricted the sale of alcohol and ordered horses to be impressed for use by the army.

The next morning Governor Augustus W. Bradford and Baltimore's Mayor John L. Chapman ordered the church bells rung to announce a proclamation declaring the city to be in imminent danger. Brigadier General Henry H. Lockwood assumed command of a civilian defense force gathering to man the existing fortifications and erect new ones where needed. Lockwood, meanwhile, ordered the streets of the city barricaded to prevent enemy cavalry from dashing through and creating mischief.[3]

The stress within the city was palpable as extreme measures were undertaken to hold the place. The *Baltimore Sun*, for example, reported that "some of the men forming companies captured citizens standing on corners and impressed them into service. This caused a general skedaddling of those who were news hunting and the result was that the streets were not much crowded during the rest of the day."[4]

Loyal men—black and white—formed militia companies, drew arms, and manned the weak line of fortifications. The city council appropriated $100,000 for the construction of new earthworks, and 400 additional policemen temporarily joined the city's force even though there was no time to issue uniforms. Instead, ribbons or badges were pinned to their clothing to denote their special status as officers of the law. The level of distress failed to subside. "The panic here is

3 One modern commentary claims that 10,000 men were mustered to defend the city from the Confederate raiders, but this seems most unlikely. Harry Wright Newman, *Maryland and the Confederacy* (Annapolis, MD: privately published, 1976), 204; *OR* 37, 2:180.

4 *Baltimore Sun*, July 11, 1864.

heavy and increasing," reported Lew Wallace early on the afternoon of July 11. It was about to get much worse.[5]

* * *

Johnson's command, located north of Frederick at Worman's Mill, set out on the arduous raid on July 9, riding east even while the battle at Monocacy was still raging. Morale was generally good, but not everyone was feeling well. In fact, Pvt. Henry C. Mettam of the 1st Maryland (Confederate) Cavalry was already in bad shape.

The trooper was suffering from an enlarged and infected gland in his groin that made riding a horse an extremely uncomfortable proposition. When he heard the expedition might pass near his family home outside Baltimore, Mettam insisted on being in the saddle for the ride. A couple of Mettam's friends carried him from his sickbed to his horse and helped him mount. "We started down the mountain, and after trotting along for some distance we all started in a run, and the place in my groin broke and went like a pistol, and the contents ran down my leg into my boots," he recorded in his diary. Later that day the men stopped at the home of one of Mettam's friends, and the man's father treated the sore. They left to return to their command with a bag of biscuits and ham and resumed the ride.[6]

Captain John P. Sheffey of the 8th Virginia Cavalry enjoyed the beauty of Maryland's piedmont region around Frederick but had nothing good to say about its inhabitants:

5 Scott Sumpter Sheads and Daniel Carroll Toomey, *Baltimore During the Civil War* (Linthicum, MD: Toomey Press, 1997), 72; *OR* 37, 2:213.

6 Samuel H. Miller, ed., "The Civil War Memoirs of the First Maryland Cavalry, C.S.A., by Henry Clay Mettam," *Maryland Historical Magazine*, 58 (1963), 156.

Bradley Johnson's cavalry occupying the town of New Windsor.

Frank Leslie's Illustrated Newspaper

> A more beautiful country never gladdened the eye of man. The horn of plenty had been outpoured upon the fields, and the land seemed burdened with its wealth of golden grain. But the people, the people, the villainous Dutch with their outlandish lingo! What a pity that they should hold so fair a land! They are nice farmers, however, and have made this portion of Maryland almost a garden. It is to be lamented that this country does not belong to Southern Sympathizers.

Sheffey went on to note that, after leaving the valley where Frederick is located, "we soon found plenty of friends—and provisions were abundantly supplied.[7]

7 Ibid.

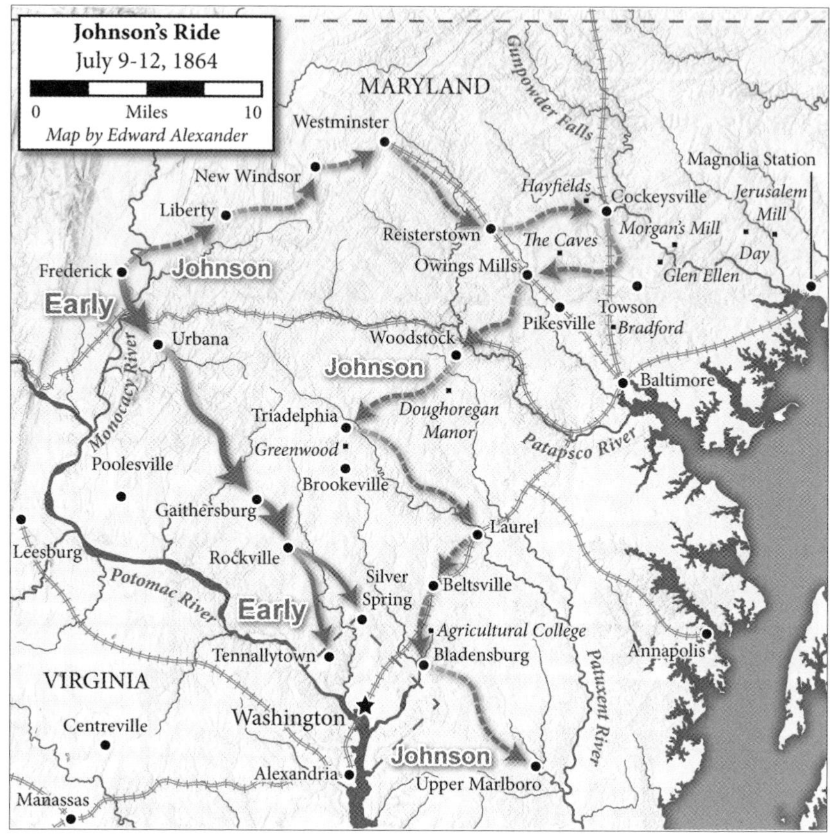

The Confederate troopers passed through Liberty, New Windsor, Westminster, and reached Reisterstown at daylight on July 10. Every store in New Windsor was closed and barred and its streets deserted. The general forced the shopkeepers to open their establishments and sell boots, shoes, and clothing to the troopers. Before departing, the Virginia horsemen set a bridge and warehouse ablaze and rode away when a Union force approached.[8]

There were about 150 Union troops in Westminster guarding the Western Maryland Railroad. Johnson ordered

8 *Carroll Record*, May-July, 1885.

Maj. Harry Gilmor, with a detachment of 20 Maryland troopers, to ride there and cut the telegraph wires. Gilmor's men dashed into Westminster with their sabers drawn screaming the Rebel yell at the top of their lungs. "The news preceded, however, that they were rebels, and it was like striking fire to tinder," said one observer. "Consternation reigned supreme."

The Maryland horsemen spotted a few Union soldiers, gave the Rebel yell again, and as curious locals peeked through drawn drapes, charged. A fair maiden waved her handkerchief at them, which increased the volume of the cheers as the gray horsemen thundered past. They cut the telegraph wires and briefly occupied the town. A courier from Johnson arrived, bringing orders to demand 1,500 suits of clothing, boots, and shoes, as a ransom. Gilmor's men also helped themselves to any available supplies of alcohol, enthusiastically "drenching their throats" with "fire-water." The town mayor was unable to gather the town council before Johnson himself arrived, but Gilmor persuaded the general to abandon the idea of burning the town.[9]

Johnson dispatched Gilmor to seize and hold the Northern Central Railway at Cockeysville.[10] While in Liberty, someone gave Gilmor a beautiful and powerful black mare, which he rode to Cockeysville. Gilmor pushed ahead of his

9 Harry Gilmor, *Four Years in the Saddle* (New York: Harper & Bros., 1866), 189-190. When Johnson moved on, his departure marked the last hostile activity in Carroll County, Maryland during the war. Nancy M. Warner, Ralph B. Levering, and Margaret Taylor Woltz. *Carroll County Maryland: A History 1837-1976* (Westminster, MD: Carroll County Bicentennial Committee, 1976), 91.

10 The Northern Central Railway connected Baltimore to Sunbury, Pennsylvania. It played an important role in the Civil War. For a detailed history of its role in the Civil War, see Scott Mingus, *Soldiers, Spies & Steam: A History of the Northern Central Railway in the Civil War* (Scotts Valley, CA: Createspace, 2016).

detachment to speak with some local friends. "I found the people everywhere took me for a Federal officer at first, not at all suspecting a rebel in that neighborhood," recalled a pleased Gilmor. "Never shall I forget the expressive countenance of one fair friend when she recognized me as I sprung from the saddle. I could only say a few words, as the column was coming up, and I must be at their head." Gilmor and his men quietly took control of the village, picketed in the direction of Baltimore, and burned the first bridge over the Gunpowder River.[11]

As the Rebel riders passed through Reisterstown, a citizen dressed in his nightclothes rushed out to make sure that the passing troops were indeed Confederates. Once he was satisfied, the man exclaimed, "Well, I told Jake so; ain't I got it on him? He thought they would never come, but I always said they would." Several hours later the same man came galloping up to the marching cavalry column to demand that Johnson return a horse taken by one of his men. He made the effort "not that he cared for the horse," explained its owner, "but that Jake would have such a rig on him. That his dear Confederates, so long expected and come at last, should take his horse!" An amused Johnson ordered the animal returned to the man.[12]

Determined to do all he could to meet the ambitious schedule for his march, Johnson kept his command moving as fast and as long as possible. "I tried to feed every six or 10 hours," he wrote years later, "slipping the horses' bridles out of their mouths and giving them enough to fill them up on the ground." His order of march, he continued, "was for the right regiment at intervals to fall out and take the rear. Marching in front rests men and horses, in the rear fatigues them." His

11 Gilmor, *Four Years in the Saddle*, 191.

12 Johnson, "My Ride Around Baltimore," 218.

was an ambitious schedule, and one sure to exhaust both men and horses alike.[13]

Johnson's main body reached Cockeysville about 9:00 a.m. on July 10. Once there, he deployed a two-gun section of the Baltimore Light Artillery under Lt. John McNulty and proceeded to burn the remaining bridges of the Northern Central Railroad, a deed that inflicted nearly $100,000 in damage to the rail line.

It was here that Johnson detached Harry Gilmor and about 150 troopers of the 1st and 2nd Maryland Cavalry Battalions to strike the bridges of the Philadelphia, Wilmington, and Baltimore Railroad spanning the Gunpowder River and destroy the lines of communication between Baltimore and the north. Gilmor was somewhat disappointed by the small number of men assigned to his excursion, for he had been led to believe his column would have as many as 500 men for the daring mission. He would have to make do with what he was assigned.[14]

While the balance of his command spent several hours in Cockeysville, Johnson dispatched "a faithful friend," Maj. James C. Clarke of the 15th Virginia Infantry, into Baltimore to ascertain the condition of the troops and forces available to defend the city.[15]

13 Johnson, "Riding a Raid."

14 Goldsborough, *The Maryland Line in the Confederate Army*, 289; Mingus, *Soldiers, Spies & Steam*, 79. Gilmor's expedition will be addressed in detail in the next chapter.

15 Major Charles Hammett Clarke, born in 1827 in Henrico County, Virginia, enlisted as a private in Company G of the 15th Virginia infantry on April 22, 1861, was commissioned a lieutenant on September 18 of that year, and captain on April 25, 1862. He was promoted to major on January 24, 1863, and was wounded at Drewry's Bluff on May 16, 1864. He was still recuperating from his wound when Johnson called on him that day. Robert K. Krick, *Lee's Colonels: A Biographical Register of the Field Officers of the Army of Northern Virginia* (Dayton, OH: Morningside House, 1992), 92. In

Johnson, meanwhile, enjoyed a pleasant lunch at "Hayfields." The place was home to his friend John Merryman, an officer in one of the militia units that had burned railroad bridges in 1861. Johnson left two lieutenants there to whom Clarke was to report. "The charming society, lovely girls, the balmy July air and the luxuriant verdure of Hayfields, all combined to make the scene enchanting to soldiers who have been for months campaigning on the battle-scarred plains and valleys of Virginia," wrote a wistful Johnson years later. What he left out was that the early-war bridge burning had prompted President Lincoln to suspend the writ of *habeas corpus* in Maryland while Merryman was arrested and imprisoned at Fort McHenry.[16]

Departing Hayfields, Johnson and his troopers moved across the Green Spring Valley in Baltimore County. "From Cockeysville, the brigade swept around Baltimore, appearing almost simultaneously on so many roads at intervals of 6 to 10 miles that many different columns were reported as advancing at once," recounted Johnson. Johnson's adjutant, Capt. George W. Booth, recalled that the approach of the

---

his postwar accounts Johnson mistakenly noted that Clarke was a colonel, but there is no evidence he reached that rank.

16 Johnson, "My Ride Around Baltimore," 219. Merryman was the subject of a landmark 1861 Supreme Court case that tested the proposition that the president of the United States could suspend *habeas corpus* during a time of rebellion: The *New York Times* described the subject litigant thusly: "Mr. Merryman is a man of family, and a gentleman of property and position, President, also, of the Maryland State Agricultural Society, and widely known and respected. He was arrested on a general order, issued for the apprehension of 'The Captain of a Secession Company in Baltimore County.'" See "Affairs in Baltimore; Habeas Corpus Case—Return of the Sheriff—Action of Chief Justice Taney; President's Instructions to Gen. Cadwallader, Suspending the Writ, Etc.," *New York Times*, May 29, 1861; Ex Parte Merryman, 17 F. Cas. 144 (C.C.D. Maryland, 1861).

Confederate cavalry caused Baltimore "to be in a great state of excitement, apprehending capture."[17]

Johnson passed his column near the country residence of Maryland Gov. Augustus W. Bradford. Retaliation was on his mind. Johnson detailed a detachment under Lt. Henry C. Blackistone (Co. B, 1st Maryland Cavalry) to burn Bradford's house as retribution for Maj. Gen. David Hunter's torching of Virginia Gov. John Letcher's Lexington home. Bradford was in Baltimore, but his family was home. The noise of soldiers on the first floor awakened some of the terrified residents. A Confederate shook Mrs. Bradford from her slumber with a knock on her bedroom door. The unnamed man handed her an order to leave the house immediately. By this time the structure already ablaze and the family had no choice but to leave with only the clothing on their backs. "Such debts required prompt payment, and this one was paid in thirty days without grace," declared an unrepentent Johnson.[18]

Johnson and his command bivouacked at and around The Caves, the home of John N. Carroll. The Caves was built in 1730 by Charles Carroll, who drafted the Declaration of Rights incorporated into the Maryland constitution.[19]

17 Johnson, "Riding a Raid"; Booth, Personal Reminiscences, 121.

18 Augustus W. Bradford to Committee on War Claims and Diary, entry for July 11, 1864, Augustus W. Bradford Papers, Maryland Historical Society, Baltimore, Maryland; Johnson, "My Ride Around Baltimore," 219; Robert J. Driver, Jr., *First and Second Maryland Cavalry* (Charlottesville, VA: Rockbridge Publishing, 1999), 200. Blackistone would be mortally wounded in combat at Bunker Hill, West Virginia, on September 9, 1864.

19 Miller, "Civil War Memoirs," 157. The Carroll family helped found the state of Maryland. Carroll would only have been 17 in the summer of 1864 and did not own the property. Johnson penned his account in 1889, when Carroll was the chief of cavalry for the Maryland National Guard and sometimes known as "General Carroll." George A. Hanson, *Old Kent: The Eastern Shore of Maryland* (Baltimore: George P. DesForges, 1876), 151.

AUGUSTUS BRADFORD

Was the governor of Maryland. His home was burned by Johnson's raiders.

Library of Congress

Private Mettam, the trooper with the infected gland in his groin, met his brother Sam there and obtained permission to pay his parents a visit. Mettam collected provisions to take with him and enjoyed a pleasant visit with family. When he tried to rejoin his command early the next morning (July 11), pickets informed the private that the brigade had left camp and was riding toward Owings' Mill. "I found them scattered along the turnpike, some lying down and some sitting up in a fence corner, sleeping. So we remained there until daybreak."[20]

About midnight, the two lieutenants left behind at Hayfields arrived in camp carrying a message from Major Clarke, who had been dispatched to gather intelligence on enemy operations. The available transportation of the Baltimore and Ohio Railroad, he explained,

> was concentrated at Locust Point . . . and the Nineteenth Corps of Grant's army, under General [William H.] Emory and part of the Sixth Corps were on transports in the stream awaiting the arrival of General Emory, to disembark, and move to Washington.

Johnson handed this critical intelligence to an officer and an escort to pass on to Jubal Early before continuing on with his ride.[21]

The march carried Johnson's troopers past Milton Painter's mill. The owner had been manufacturing ice cream

20 Miller, "Civil War Memoirs," 157. Today, Owings' Mill is a suburb of Baltimore.

21 Johnson, "My Ride Around Baltimore," 219. According to Johnson's published account, these were two separate instances. While bivouacked at The Caves, "I at once sent this information to General Early by an officer and escort, and moved on." After passing Doughregan Manor on the afternoon of July 11, noted Johnson, "I dispatched another message to General Early by a trusty courier, guided by the son of a friend, who undertook to show him the way across the country."

since before the outbreak of the Civil War, and there was a large supply of the frozen treat on hand. In fact, workers were loading a train car with freezers of ice cream to be shipped to market in Baltimore when the gray troopers reached the scene. "As rations were scarce and issued with great irregularity, the ice cream was confiscated and issued to the troops, many of whom had never seen anything like it," recalled Johnson. "The mountaineers thought that the 'beer' was nice, but too cold, so they put it in their canteens to melt." Others, calling it "frozen mush," dumped the flavored delicacy into their hats and ate it with their hands. Private Mettam and his friends took possession of a ten-gallon freezer, "and with the cakes I had brought from home, we were soon having a cold free lunch for breakfast."[22]

"It was a most ludicrous sight to see the ice cream dished out into all conceivable receptacles, and the whole brigade engaged in feasting on this, to many, a novel luxury as the column moved along," recorded Johnson's adjutant Captain Booth. He was so amused by what he saw that he left a detailed description of the event. "The men," he continued.

> carried it in hats, rubber blankets, in buckets and old tin cans—in fact, anything that would hold the cream was utilized. No spoons were at hand, but as fingers and hands were made before spoons, the natural and primary organs were brought into play. A number of the men from southwest Virginia were not familiar with this delicious food, but were not slow in becoming acquainted with its enticing properties and expressing themselves as being very much satisfied with the 'frozen vittles,' as they termed it.[23]

22 Johnson, "My Ride Around Baltimore," 220. One can only imagine the expressions on the faces of these cavalrymen as the experienced "brain freeze" for the first time. Johnson, "Riding a Raid"; Miller, "Civil War Memoirs," 157.

23 Booth, *Personal Reminiscences*, 124.

A handful of troopers of Company E of the 8th Virginia Cavalry were enjoying their "frozen mush" when some of their comrades from Company C, who had liberated a quantity of Dutch cheese and were enjoying it when they trotted past, offered a trade. Everyone involved enjoyed a particularly savory breakfast that morning.[24]

Once they moved out again, the column trotted past a large girls' school. Their professor and matrons tried to control the young ladies, but failed miserably. "Every southern girl was over the fence and lined up cheering us as we passed and any lucky knight knew they would have to dismount and the whole line would kiss him after an introduction," wrote James D. Sedinger, a member of Company E of the 8th Virginia Cavalry, in his diary. "It made for braver men of the boys after witnessing the scenes at that school; the devotion of the Southern girls to the cause." Not all service in the field was an ordeal.[25]

The horse soldiers continued riding on until they struck the Baltimore & Ohio Railroad above Woodstock. They suffered a few casualties, including a young lieutenant who was killed.[26]

Proceeding on, the column passed by Doughoregan Manor, the home of John Lee Carroll near Ellicott City in Howard County, another member of the prominent Carroll family. Johnson stopped there for lunch. That afternoon the general detailed another courier to carry a message to

24 Jack L. Dickinson, 8*th Virginia Cavalry* (Lynchburg, VA: H. E. Howard, 1986), 49.

25 James D. Sedinger, "Diary of a Border Ranger," entry for July 11, 1864, West Virginia State Archives, Charleston, West Virginia.

26 Johnson, "Riding a Raid." The obviously brief engagement is something of a mystery and Johnson does not otherwise mention or describe it in his more heavily referenced "My Ride Around Baltimore" article.

General Early, this one helped along by the son of a friend who guided the courier across Baltimore County.[27]

After defeating Wallace at Monocacy, Jubal Early resumed his advance towards the capital at Washington. Unfortunately for Early, the victory at Monocacy also cost him precious time. It took him nearly two days to arrive at Silver Spring on the outskirts of Washington, where Early waited to test the lightly-guarded fortifications. While the Confederates recovered from a month of hard marching and excessive heat, reinforcements from the Union VI Corps and XIX Corps arrived via steamship.

As Early's men probed the Federal works at Fort Stevens on July 11, sustained skirmishing lasted into the night. It was then that Johnson's message reached Early. "During the night," recalled, the Confederate commander,

> a dispatch was received from General Bradley Johnson from near Baltimore, informing me that he had received information from a reliable source that two army corps had arrived from General Grant's army and that his whole army was probably in motion. This caused me to delay the attack [on Fort Stevens] until I could examine the works again, and as soon as it was light enough to see, I rode to the front and found the parapets lined with troops. I had therefore, reluctantly, to give up all hopes of capturing Washington after I had arrived in sight of the dome of the capital and given the Federal authorities a terrible fright.[28]

27 Johnson, "My Ride Around Baltimore," 220. John Lee Carroll was the great-grandson of Charles Carroll of Carrollton, founder of Maryland, the last surviving signer of the Declaration of Independence. Carroll, a prominent Harvard-trained attorney and politician, was elected governor of Maryland in 1867, serving two four-year terms. "John Lee Carroll," Archives of Maryland Biographical Series: https://tinyurl.com/bdk8y36b.

28 Golsborough, *The Maryland Line in the Confederate Army*, 205; Early, *A Memoir of the Last Year of the War of Independence in the Confederate States of America*, 62-63.

Convinced that any assault would meet with heavy losses, Early began withdrawing his troops on the evening of July 12. The immediate threat to Washington had subsided.

* * *

While Early was deciding whether to assault the works at Fort Stevens, Johnson and his brigade continued their rapid ride toward Point Lookout, moving through the lovely rolling country along the undulating boundary dividing Howard and Montgomery counties.

The Rebel horsemen crossed the Patuxent River and reached the village of Triadelphia near Brookeville in Montgomery County about nine that night. Johnson unsaddled and fed his horse and allowed his weary troopers to do the same. Everyone needed sleep. He and his officers dined at Greenwood, the nearby home of businessman and slave owner Allen Bowie Davis. Their respite was short-lived. About midnight, word reached Johnson that a large force of Union horse soldiers of Brig. Gen. James H. Wilson's Third Cavalry Division, Army of the Potomac, had established their camps at Brookeville just a few miles away. In other words, the Union authorities knew about the presence of his Confederate troopers. "I at once got ready and began to attack them," recorded Johnson, "but on reaching that point found they too had received information of their unwelcome neighbors and had left."[29]

Disappointed, Johnson and his column marched to Beltsville in Prince George's County, a stop on the railroad between Baltimore and Washington, about seven miles north of the boundary of the District of Columbia. He planned to

29 Johnson, "My Ride Around Baltimore," 221.

cross and tear up the Washington branch of the B & O Railroad near Laurel.[30]

After determining they lacked sufficient force to destroy the Baltimore & Ohio line, the Confederate troopers satisfied themselves by cutting the telegraph wire and attempting to set fire to the railroad bridge over Paint Branch, a creek two and a half miles southeast of Beltsville. The fire was set in haste, however, and burned itself out without doing any damage to the bridge. While the raiders were at the B & O depot at Beltsville, one of them confided to a railroad employee that the Rebels were worried that they would be cut off or overwhelmed by a superior enemy force. Some of the raiders looted a nearby store in Beltsville, offering payment in Confederate dollars, which the loyal shopkeeper declined to accept.[31]

The main body of Johnson's column arrived at Beltsville early on the morning of July 12. There, they found Wilson's troopers, who had been dismounted as a result of the severe losses they had sustained during the unsuccessful Wilson-Kautz Raid into south-central Virginia from June 22 to July 1. The advance guard fired on Union pickets, killing one man and wounding another. The gunfire stirred up a hornet's nest of activity within the ranks of the Yankee cavalrymen. The blue-clad veterans were mounted on horses unaccustomed to the travails of cavalry service, which rendered them unreliable and severely hindered the effectiveness of Wilson's men.[32]

Johnson deployed Lieutenant McNulty's two guns, which promptly opened fire. Supported by the artillery, Johnson's

30 Ibid.

31 "The Raiders.; How Bradley Johnson was Captured and Escaped the Raid in Maryland. Strength of the Rebel Force," *New York Times*, July 19, 1864.

32 Ibid.

attack drove the Federals down the road toward Bladensburg in what proved to be a short fight. Not far from Bladensburg, the Confederate cavalry found several hundred government mules that would do nicely to mount the prisoners they expected to free at Point Lookout. Johnson had the animals rounded up and secured, after which the men stopped to feed their horses and the mules.[33]

Johnson, however, was not moving fast enough. He was already a full twenty-four hours behind schedule and his horses were already jaded. After the delay caused by the skirmish with Wilson's men and wrangling the mules, Johnson realized that he still had nearly 90 miles to cover to get to Point Lookout by that night—as he had been ordered to do. "It was physically impossible for men to make the ride in the time designated," declared Johnson. "I determined, however, to come as near it as possible."[34]

He instructed his trusted adjutant, Capt. George W. Booth, to take a detachment of men from the 1st Maryland Cavalry who were knowledgeable about the area and ride as quickly as possible around the nearby countryside to impress horses from residents along the route to Point Lookout. "They were unanimously my friends," wrote Johnson, "and I requested them to have their horses on the roadside, so that I could exchange my broken down animals for their fresh ones, and thus borrow them for the occasion." This was a brilliant plan, and it offered the only opportunity for Johnson to complete his assigned mission.

Johnston later explained how it all worked:

> During the preceding day, I had been taking horses by flankers on each side of my column, and kept a supply of fresh ones at the rear of each

33 Booth, *Personal Reminiscences*, 124.

34 Johnson, "My Ride Around Baltimore," 221-222; Goldsborough, *The Maryland Line in the Confederate Army*, 289.

> regiment. As soon as a man's horse broke down, he fell out of the ranks, waited until the rest of his regiment came up, got a fresh horse, left his old one, and resumed his place.[35]

This scheme allowed his command to move at a trot instead of at a walk, which was otherwise impossible for a cavalry column to do for any extended period of time; it was too tiring to the horses without breaking them down. There was, however, a downside to this scheme, and it would take some time for the problem to surface. "The horses left behind," admitted Johnson, "were well bred mounts from Southwest Virginia, and far better than the overfed, fat, pudgy horses that we got, these last could not stand over 20 miles march."[36]

After returning from the pursuit of Wilson's routed troopers, Johnson turned toward Upper Marlboro, determined to get as close to Point Lookout as possible. The column had only covered a short distance when a courier from General Early overtook the command. The rider carried an order directing Johnson to report to Early at army headquarters on the Seventh Street Road in Silver Spring, Maryland. Johnson obeyed the order and marched his brigade along the Seventh Street Road until it reached the campus of the Maryland Agricultural College.

Henry Onderdonk, the Agricultural College's president, warmly welcomed the newly arrived Confederate cavalrymen and had his kitchen staff go out of their way to feed them. Johnson established his headquarters at a nearby manor home, which triggered longstanding rumors that he held a

35 Johnson, "My Ride Around Baltimore," 222.

36 Johnson, "Riding a Raid."

The original building of the Maryland Agricultural College, which burned down in 1912.

Library of Congress

gala that night with a number of the local ladies in attendance.[37]

37 Daniel Carroll Toomey, *The Civil War in Maryland* (Baltimore: Toomey Press, 1983), 127-129. After Early's raid ended, the Federal government conducted an investigation to ascertain how the kitchen at the Agricultural College managed to feed hundreds of Confederate soldiers when the college was not in session during the summer months. Congressman John A. Bingham of Ohio, a Radical Republican, was appointed as Judge Advocate of the U.S. Army with the rank of major by President Lincoln. In late July 1864, Bingham issued an order for the immediate arrest of Henry Onderdonk, who was forced to resign as a result how he treated Johnson and his men. Turner-Baker Papers, Case #4089, "Henry Onderdonk," NARA. The Agricultural College is known today as the University of Maryland.

While he was near the college campus Johnson somehow lost his prized Colt revolver, one of the largest and most expensive made by the legendary manufacturer. A young man named O. H. Norton, of Madison, Wisconsin, found the revolver in the woods near the college early on the morning of the 13th. Johnson apparently realized that the gun was missing, because he sent one of his troopers back to find it; the soldier had failed to locate it in the inky darkness.[38]

"I moved down the Washington road to the Agricultural College, and thence along the line of the Federal pickets, marching all night, occasionally driving in a picket, and expecting every moment to be fired upon from the works, within range of which I was moving," recollected the brigadier. "By dark," remembered Booth, "we were skirting the outer lines of earthworks around Washington, but the night concealed our movements and were not molested. This circumstance was most favorable," he continued, "as in the narrow roads our column of some 1200 or 1300 men, together with our battery the ordnance wagons and ambulances, made quite an extended line, and this was aggravated by the captured mules, which we were driving along, loose, in the road."

Booth took the advance and sent men out to picket each road to Washington intersecting their line of march. The pickets frequently drew the fire of the forts along the way. Johnson's troopers could not have made that movement during the day because, fully visible, the Federal forts would have shot them to pieces. Booth and his advance group reached General Early about nine that evening. Early, who was mounted and watching the passage of his infantry,

38 "Bradley Johnston's Pistol," *New York Times*, July 31, 1864.

directed that the cavalry halt until the infantry had passed, at which time the horsemen were to protect his rear.[39]

Despite all of the alarm raised and chaos caused, Johnson nevertheless managed to pass by the entirety of the northeast front of Washington's defenses unscathed. It was a daring ride carried to a successful conclusion because of Johnson's bold and capable management.[40]

Early's orders to Johnson were to close up the rear with Brig. Gen. William L. "Mudwall" Jackson's cavalry brigade following along behind him. Johnson's horsemen reached Rockville during the day on July 13, where they found Jackson and his men skirmishing with troopers of the 2nd Massachusetts Cavalry, which hung on his rear and "rendered things very uncomfortable generally," as Johnson put it.[41]

He ordered a charge to support "Mudwall's men, driving the enemy and capturing a number of them. Captain Nicholas of the 1st Maryland Cavalry, the acting inspector general of the Maryland Line, led the charge of the first squadron. His horse was shot out from under him, and the captain was also shot and taken prisoner. "He was as good a soldier and as gallant a gentleman as ever rode a horse in that war," Johnson declared.[42]

The charge also cost another man—Johnson himself. His horse took a round in the leg and went lame. Federals quickly

39 Booth, *Personal Reminiscences*, 125.

40 Gilmor, *Four Years in the Saddle*, 203. Gilmor and his returning raiders had caught up to Johnson's command about two miles south of Poolesville at daylight on July 13, and the reunited column had moved to join Early and the main body of the army as ordered.

41 Johnson, "My Ride Around Baltimore," 222.

42 Bradley T. Johnson, "The Maryland Line," included in Clement A. Evans, ed., *Confederate Military History*, 12 vols. (Atlanta: Confederate Publishing Co., 1899), 2:123.

ROBERT RANSOM
The major general led the cavalry division assigned to Jubal Early's Army of the Valley.
Museum of the Confederacy

surrounded the now-dismounted soldier, not knowing their prisoner was a general officer and the leader of the Rebel horse brigade. He was being escorted to the rear in the company of two Yankee troopers when some of his Marylanders made a desperate and successful mounted charge to rescue him. With Johnson safely back in their ranks, the Rebels broke off and withdrew. As they did so, they blocked the road with brush, logs and broken wagons to discourage pursuit by the Yankees.[43]

"During the rest of the 13th our pursuers treated us with more respect," Johnson noted. "The men marched and stopped periodically all night that night, with that terrible, tedious delay and iteration so wearing to men and horses, and it was not until Thursday, the 14th, we reached Poolesville." Arriving there, Johnson received orders to act as the army's rear guard while the infantry and artillery crossed the Potomac. He deployed a skirmish line, unlimbered his artillery, and checked the pursuit of the Federals for several hours. "At last, in the afternoon, a wide line of skirmishers could be seen stretching far beyond each flank of those we

43 "The Raiders."

had been engaged with and which moved forward with a steady alignment, very unusual for dismounted cavalry." Jackson's Virginia brigade "covered the retreat fighting the cavalry to Poolville (sic)," recounted James D. Sedinger of the 8th Virginia Cavalry. "The regiment was dismounted and deployed as skirmishers and from 10 A.M. until dark held the enemy in check."[44]

Johnson asked his division commander, Maj. Gen. Robert Ransom, Jr., to visit his position because the enemy infantry had arrived, and it was time for the cavalry to depart. Ransom soon joined him, and together they watched the advancing line of the enemy through their field glasses. There was no mistaking the sound of infantry weapons for cavalry carbines. "We mounted and started for the Potomac," recounted Sedinger of the 8th Virginia in his diary, "was halted and told to lay down with our horses fastened to us to be ready for any emergency."[45]

According to Johnson, the Rebels made "a great show with our artillery and repeatedly attempting to charge with cavalry, so that we delayed them until their supports could deploy." By this time the enemy had advanced some distance and the time to move out had arrived. Once Johnson was "notified that everything, including my own baggage and ordnance train had crossed, I withdrew comfortably and got into Virginia about sundown."[46]

"We had been marching, fighting and working, from daylight July 9th until sundown July 14th, four days and a half, or about one hundred and eight hours," proudly declared Johnson in 1889. "We had unsaddled only twice

44 Johnson, "My Ride Around Baltimore," 223; Sedinger, entry for July 13, 1864.

45 Sedinger, .entry for July 14, 1864.

46 Johnson, "My Ride Around Baltimore," 223.

during that time, *with a halt of from four to five hours each time*, making nearly one hundred hours of marching. We had isolated Baltimore from the North," continued the proud former soldier, "and cut off Washington from the United States, having made a circuit from Frederick to Cockeysville on the east, to Beltsville on the south, and through Rockville and Poolesville on the west."[47]

Johnson, however, only managed to get about 100 miles from Point Lookout before turning back. Whatever he had managed to accomplish, it was not his mission. He had failed to free a single prisoner at Point Lookout. The attempt, which in fairness to Johnson was never a viable plan, was the victim of an impossible schedule, the two-day delay getting the orders for the ill-fated expedition into Johnson's hands, and Grant's decision to send troops to reinforce the defenses of Washington.

Harry Gilmor's expedition, by comparison, reached its objectives: the railroad bridges over the Gunpowder River.

47 Ibid.

Chapter 6

Harry Gilmor's Ride

BRIGADIER GENERAL Bradley T. Johnson selected Maj. Harry Gilmor to lead the expedition to destroy the railroad bridges over the Gunpowder River to the north of the City of Baltimore.

Harry Ward Gilmor was indeed a child of privilege. He born on January 24, 1838, at "Glen Ellen," a 1,000-acre estate near Towson, Maryland. The home was a handsome Tudor-style mansion owned by his father Robert Gilmor, III, a prominent merchant and importer of goods. Glen Ellen was designed to be a replica of Sir Walter Scott's castle in Scotland and featured high mullioned windows and battlemented towers.[1]

Harry, the fifth of eleven children, worked in the family importing business before the outbreak of the Civil War. The big and burly Gilmor was a bit more than six feet tall, dark

1 Glen Ellen was constructed in 1833 at a cost of $175,000.00, which would equate to about $5.3 million today. By 1929, Glen Ellen was decaying and in poor condition, so it was demolished. Katherine Drew DeBoalt, "Once There was a Castle," *Baltimore Sun*, June 6, 1993.

HARRY W. GILMOR

The dashing lieutenant colonel led the expedition to destroy the railroad bridges over the Gunpowder River.

Library of Congress

complected, sported flashing blue eyes, and had a picaresque character.

Gilmor was arrested as a spy in Baltimore in August 1861, held prisoner for two weeks, and released. If there was ever any doubt about his loyalties, they ended when he enlisted as a private in Company G of the 7th Virginia Cavalry on August 31, 1861. He was promoted to sergeant major and helped to organize Company F of the 12th Virginia Cavalry. After being elected captain of that company on April 10, 1862, he served in Thomas J. "Stonewall" Jackson's 1862 Valley Campaign and then participated in Brig. Gen. Albert G. Jenkins' raid into western Virginia. Gilmor was captured at Reisterstown, Maryland, on September 12 while visiting his family and charged with spying. The charge could have brought the death penalty, but he was instead held in Baltimore's Fort McHenry until his exchange on February 13, 1863.[2]

The Maryland native returned to duty, briefly served on the staff of Maj. Gen. J. E. B. Stuart, and was present at the March 17, 1863, Battle of Kelly's Ford. He resigned on May 7 to raise and organize the 2nd Battalion of Maryland Cavalry for service as partisan rangers. According to Robert J. Driver, Jr., the modern historian of the 2nd Maryland, "The history of the Second Maryland Cavalry begins and ends with Harry Gilmor."[3]

A promotion to major was forthcoming on May 27 and he participated in the Gettysburg Campaign while commanding both the 1st and 2nd Maryland Cavalry. During the invasion he served as provost marshal for the town of Gettysburg from July 1-4, 1863. That fall, Gilmor was wounded in the leg in

2 Gilmor, *Four Years in the Saddle*, 61.

3 Robert J. Driver. Jr., *First & Second Maryland Cavalry, C.S.A.* (Rockbridge Publishing), 145.

fighting at Charles Town, West Virginia on October 15. His battalion of partisan rangers was mustered into regular service with the Confederate cavalry on May 5, and Gilmor led his troopers at the Battle of New Market that day. He was wounded once more, this time in the back, at Mt. Jackson, Virginia, on May 12, but recovered in time to fight at Piedmont on June 5. When Bradley Johnson assumed command of William "Grumble" Jones's cavalry brigade after Piedmont, Gilmor and his 2nd Maryland Cavalry officially joined Johnson's Brigade.[4]

According to another famous Maryland Confederate, Maj. Henry Kyd Douglas, Gilmor didn't think all that much of his officer's commission. "He was just as likely to use it to light a pipe as to have preserved it or taken any care of it," claimed Douglas.[5]

Fearless, dashing, and an inspirational leader of men, Harry Gilmor in many ways the beau ideal of a cavalryman. The fact that he hailed from the area that was the object of the expedition meant he knew it well. That made him the best possible choice among the officers of Johnson's command to lead the expedition to the Gunpowder River.[6]

* * *

The Gunpowder River is a 6.8-mile tidal estuary on the western side of the Chesapeake Bay in northern Maryland. The estuary is formed by the junction of two freshwater rivers, Gunpowder Falls and Little Gunpowder Falls. The

4 Driver, *First and Second Maryland Cavalry*, 145, 318

5 Goldsborough, *The Maryland Line in the Confederate Army*, 241.

6 Driver, *First and Second Maryland Cavalry*, 145 and 318. For a full-length biography of Gilmor, see Timothy Ackinclose, *Sabres & Pistols: The Civil War Career of Colonel Harry Gilmor, G.S.A.: The Civil War Career of Colonel Harry Gilmor, C.S.A.* (Baltimore: Butternut & Blue, 1997).

One of the bridges of the Philadelphia, Wilmington & Baltimore Railroad over the Gunpowder River as it appeared in 1869.

Library of Congress

bridge over Gunpowder River is about two miles below Magnolia Station, a stop on the Philadelphia, Wilmington & Baltimore Railroad (the "PW&B") near the historic community of Joppa. It was just 15 miles north of Baltimore and about 50 miles southwest of Wilmington, Delaware. The river's name came about because saltpeter, a crucial ingredient in the manufacture of gunpowder, was discovered along its banks in 1665. The area has strategic significance because of its ready access to the Chesapeake Bay.[7]

7 "History of the Gunpowder River," www.greatfeathers.com/overview-history-maryland.

Johnson's orders were for Gilmor to burn the bridges of the PW&B across the Back, Gunpowder, and Bush rivers, each of which were defended by contingents of Union troops. Concerned about the security of those important railroad bridges, on May 23 Lew Wallace had ordered Brig. Gen. John R. Kenly to post detachments to guard them. Gilmor knew these spans were not unattended, "but with my slender force, I could not be sanguine of a favorable result." As Gilmor later reported, "General Johnson said he could spare no more men, and feared to trust artillery so far away from support, and also said that he was obliged to keep a large portion of my command with him as scouts and guides."[8]

Gilmor and his small command left Cockeysville about noon and moved out as if they were headed for Baltimore. Gilmor soon changed course toward Towson and, finding no enemy, went straight to a bridge at another point on the Gunpowder.

As early as July 10, Federal authorities were aware of the Confederate foray into northern Maryland. "Repeated reports confirm the presence of the enemy on the York Road at Cockeysville and Towsontown, variously estimated from 1,600 to 1,700," reported Bvt. Brig. Gen. W. W. Morris, commanding troops in Baltimore, to the War Department's inspector general. He continued:

> All reports tend to the theory that a force intends to cut the Philadelphia [rail]road. The report of the destruction of the Gunpowder bridge on the Northern Central road is reliable, I think. I have sent two small steamers to the Gunpowder and Bush River bridges, one to each, with a howitzer. Major Judd, at Wilmington, was instructed to

8 *OR* 37, 1:530; Gilmor, *Four Years in the Saddle*, 192. For a study of the role played by the PW&B during the Civil War, see Scott L. Mingus, Sr. and Robert L. Williams, *"This Trying Hour": The Philadelphia, Wilmington & Baltimore Railroad in the Civil War* (Scotts Valley, CA: Makespace, 2017).

> strengthen the infantry guards at the bridges named. He reports that he has done so. General Cadwalader, at my request, said he would try and send a battery from Philadelphia to further protect the bridges.[9]

That same day, a correspondent for a local newspaper reported to Secretary of the Navy Gideon Welles that the Confederates had cut the Northern Central Railroad at Cockeysville and at Texas, Maryland, and that Gilmor and his command were headed toward the nearly mile-long PW&B drawbridge over the Gunpowder River. Welles immediately

9 OR 37, 2:176. Morris was wrong about the destruction of the bridge.

ordered three gunboats to the disputed area—one to Havre de Grace and one each to the railroad bridges over the Bush and Gunpowder rivers. He also ordered the frigate U.S.S. *Minnesota* to Point Lookout and four more gunboats to the Potomac River from Hampton Roads.[10]

Northern officials readily identified the object of Gilmor's expedition. "It is now confidently believed [the Confederate cavalry] are making for the Philadelphia, Wilmington and Baltimore railroad to endeavor to cut it, and destroy the bridges," reported the *Washington Evening Star* on July 11. As if to emphasize that there was nothing to fear, it added, "This is merely a small cavalry raid, and the impression prevails that the main body of rebels have gone toward Annapolis Junction." The *New York Times* chimed in the following day, noting that "fears are entertained that a number of mills, factories and foundries around [Baltimore] will be destroyed."[11]

Major Henry B. Judd was a 45-year-old Regular Army veteran and had seen service in the Mexican War. He was a member of the West Point class of 1839 and had seen continuous service for the 25 years between his graduation and the events of July 1864. His promotion to major of the 4th U.S. Artillery arrived in 1861, just as the war was getting underway, but he retired from active service soon thereafter because of disability. He was in charge of the Union

10 *NOR* 5:458-459.

11 "Cutting the Railroads," *Washington Evening Star*, July 11, 1864; "The Excitement in Baltimore—The Burning of Gunpowder Bridge—Destruction of Gov. Bradford's House—An Act of Retaliation," *New York Times*, July 12, 1864.

recruiting office at Wilmington, Delaware, that fourth summer of the war.[12]

On July 10, just as Gilmor's raid was getting underway, headquarters advised Judd that "The force of the enemy sent to cut the railroad between this and Wilmington is known to be small." Judd took this at face value and ordered 100 convalescent soldiers from the Veteran Reserve Corps under Lt. James Lewis to report at Havre de Grace to protect the ferryboat and railroad property there.[13]

Judd also had an entire regiment of thirty-days' militia, the 7th Delaware Infantry, available for use. Fifty men of the 7th Delaware under Capt. Thomas H. Stirling reinforced a detachment guarding the drawbridge over the Gunpowder River near Magnolia Station. Lieutenant Robert Price and 32 men of Company F of the 159th Regiment, Ohio National Guard, were already guarding the southern end of the drawbridge. According to Price, his men "were almost worn out with constant watching, and that I thought something was going wrong near here, but I had not the men to investigate." Stirling's Delaware men arrived at 3:00 a.m. on July 10 and took up a position on the northern end of the

12 George Washington Cullum, *Biographical Register of the Officers and Graduates of the U.S. Military Academy at West Point, New York*, 3 vols. (New York: D. Van Nostrand, 1868), 2:560-561.

13 *OR* 37, 2:184. The Veteran Reserve Corps was a military organization created during the Civil War to permit partially disabled or convalescent soldiers to perform light duty in order to free up able-bodied soldiers for service in the field. According to an 1865 newspaper article: "The men in this corps are such as have been partially disabled in service, but who still retain sufficient health and limbs to perform garrison duty and numerous other military labors which will yet for a long time be needed." More than 60,000 men served in the Veteran Reserve Corps from its formation until the conclusion of the Civil War. "Value and Economy of the Veteran Reserve Corps," *New York Times*, October 6, 1865.

span. Roughly 82 officers and men of dubious quality and state of rest guarded the important bridge.[14]

The Confederate cavalry fanned out across the countryside, gathering horses and collecting information. The sight of Rebels in this area was somewhat novel, as most of the local residents were Union sympathizers. "We will do these men the credit to say they behaved themselves remarkably well," noted a local newspaper. "They destroyed nothing and took nothing but what they were willing and able to pay for. The extent of their purchases were two hats."[15]

Gilmor left Capt. James R. Bayley in command there and, taking a few officers and men, rode over to see his family at Glen Ellen. "I captured the whole party on the front steps when I rode up," joked Gilmor, "and—if I except some, perhaps just complaint of my rather severe hugging—treated them with kindness, and upon detainment for a few hours, paroled and released them, and moved on with my command." When Gilmor revealed his objective to a family member, the relative "uttered the not very cheering prediction that I would never return alive." Gilmor admitted that he was "much of the same opinion myself, seeing the insignificant force I had. But I resolved to fight and whip ever thing I came across in that neighborhood."[16]

Despite the fact that his men were exhausted by long days in the saddle and very much in want of sleep, Gilmor kept his column moving even as night came upon them. He took the road through the Dulany Valley, intending to cross a bridge over the Gunpowder River near Morgan's Mill. He was so tired that fell asleep in the saddle and did not wake until he arrived at a gate where barking dogs roused him from his

14 *OR* 37, 1:225, 230; *NOR* 5: 458-459.

15 *Baltimore County Advocate*, July 16, 1864.

16 Gilmor, *Four Years in the Saddle*, 192.

uncomfortable slumber. His untimely nap compelled him to cross the Gunpowder farther up. Just as their commander had done, many of his riders had nodded off in the saddle and some had even toppled from their horses. Given the size of his command, Gilmor could not afford to lose any men from any cause during the march. He decided it was best to bivouac on a nearby farm until daylight so his men could get some desperately needed sleep.[17]

Gilmor roused his men at daybreak. When they moved out, Ordnance Sgt. Eugene W. Field and another man led the advance because the colonel was not expecting any trouble in the area. The men cut some telegraph wires as the column continued. When a shot rang out ahead, Gilmor and four men put spurs to their horses and dashed forward to investigate. They met the trooper who had accompanied Field on the way back so rapidly that Gilmor thought he had seen the enemy ahead. The man told Gilmor that Field was dead, and when Gilmor reached the house of 75-year-old Ishmael Day, he found Field lying on the ground with his face and chest filled with buckshot—but still alive. Field told Gilmor that he had ordered Day to take down a large U.S. flag he was flying outside his home, that that Day had refused to do so. The irrate landowner then carried out Maj. Gen. John A. Dix 1861 exhortation: "If any man attempts to haul down the American flag, shoot him on the spot!" When Field dismounted to haul the flag down himself, Day seized a shotgun and unloaded it into Field at point-blank range. Day later claimed that he shot Field because he called the flag "a damned old rag."[18]

Some of Gilmor's men searched for Day, who had escaped into the nearby woods, while Gilmor tended to Field. Others

17 Ibid., 192-193.

18 "The Magnolia Raid," *New York Times*, July 14, 1864; Neal A. Brooks and Erlc G. Rockel, *A History of Baltimore County* (Towson, MD: Friends of the Towson Library, Inc., 1979), 248.

A woodcut depicting Harry Gilmor's cavalry raid on Magnolia Station.

Frank Leslie's Illustrated Newspaper

satisfied themselves by setting Day's house, barn, and outbuildings ablaze. "Scarcely ever had I seen men so excited," admitted Gilmor, "and I am sure that it would have been out of my power to save Day had they caught him." Field knew that he was dying, and he also knew that Gilmor could not linger with him. He begged him not to let his mortal wounding jeopardize the mission. Gilmor gave him water from a tin cup and received his dying messages, including telling the colonel where to find some papers that Field had hidden. Gilmor had the dying man loaded into one of Day's carriages and carried to a nearby hotel. Field died soon thereafter at the age of 34.[19]

Mrs. Day would later complain bitterly about the theft of money and silver and the burning of her house by "Glen Ellen's aristocractic son." To her it demonstrated the lack of a a proper upbringing. "Had his father taught him the art of handling the plough, perhaps he would not have become a highway robber," she indignantly declared. Only a small

19 Gilmor, *Four Years in the Saddle*, 194-194.

outbuilding survived the flames. A month later, Day sold his remaining property.[20]

The troopers moved on, soon arriving at David Lee's Jerusalem Mill. They requisitioned horses and whatever they could carry away from Lee's store, including boots, shoes, and riding apparel. Including stolen grain from Magnolia Station, Lee reported that the visit by Gilmor and his troopers cost him $1,000.00. The Rebels, meanwhile, pressed on and destroyed telegraph lines along three different roads.[21]

Gilmor's small column was within a mile and a half of the railroad bridge where the PW&B crossed the Gunpowder River when a passenger train was spotted coming from the direction of Baltimore. Gilmor ordered Captain Bayley and 20 troopers to dash ahead and capture the train, which they soon accomplished. Guards surrounded the rail cars and strict orders were issued against plundering of any kind. Gilmor threatened to shoot or cut down the first man he saw doing anything of the sort. The major also assigned a guard to the baggage master, who was instructed to deliver to each passenger their personal property and then unload the train. Unfortunately, lamented Gilmor, the engineer crippled the locomotive before escaping in the chaos, "or I should have run up to Havre de Grace, and made an effort to burn all the bridges, and likewise the large steamer there."[22]

20 Brooks and Rockel, A History of Baltimore County, 249-250. The episode made Day became something of a folk hero. Organizations issued resolutions of sympathy, and financial aid flowed in from staunch Unionists. Day relocated to Baltimore, where he held a position as inspector at the Customs House. He died of pneumonia on December 26, 1873, at the age of 83. Ibid., 253.

21 *The Harford County Correspondent*, July 12, 1864; Harry Gilmor to George Booth, July 28, 1864, Harry Gilmor Papers, 1862-1865, Archives Maryland Historical Society, Baltimore, Maryland.

22 Gilmor, *Four Years in the Saddle*, 194.

WILLIAM B. FRANKLIN

The former corps commander and one of the highest-ranking officers in the Union army was briefly held as a prisoner by Harry Gilmor.

Library of Congress

In addition to the civilians, about 20 uniformed Union officers were on board. To Gilmor's surprise and delight, one of his men told him that a major general named William Buel Franklin was a passenger. Franklin was not just any general, but one of the highest ranking officers in the Federal service.

The 1843 West Point graduate had ranked first in his class, which also included Ulysses S. Grant. He saw service in the Mexican War, began the Civil War as a colonel, soon made general, and led an infantry corps in several major campaigns with the Army of the Potomac, including on the Peninsula, Antietam, and at Fredericksburg. He was recovering from a combat wound suffered at the Battle of Mansfield that spring in Louisiana during the Red River Campaign. Franklin was on his way north to convalesce when Gilmor stopped the train. "I was suspicious of an attack upon the [rail]road that day," Franklin later told his sister, "and took the earliest train because I gained an hour at the dangerous end of the road by taking it."[23]

After the train safely crossed the drawbridge and headed for Magnolia Station, Franklin heaved a sigh of relief, "and I imagined the danger was over. I was in citizen's dress, and flattered myself that I would not be recognized." He was wrong. A Confederate spy was on board. Although he did not

23 Franklin had been found partially responsible for the debacle that befell the Army of the Potomac at Fredericksburg, a determination that crippled his career. He was commanding the XIX Corps in the ill-fated Red River Campaign of 1864, when he was wounded. He had a successful post-Army career as general manager of Colt's Fire Army Manufacturing Company, supervised the construction of the Connecticut state capital building, was a presidential elector for Samuel J. Tilden in 1876, and served as commissioner general of the United States for the Paris Exposition of 1888. He died in Hartford, Connecticut on May 8, 1903, and was buried in his hometown of York, Pennsylvania. Warner, *Generals in Blue*, 159-160. For a full-length biography of Franklin, see Mark A. Snell, *From First to Last: The Life of William B. Franklin* (New York: Fordham University Press, 2002).

recognize Franklin, he knew the general was also on the train and reported his presence.[24]

Intrigued, Gilmor entered the car pointed out to him, and asked some of the uniformed officers aboard it who was General Franklin. No one responded, so Gilmor personally examined each of the passenger's papers until he came to Franklin. The general later explained he was concerned that Gilmor would read his papers, one of which "would have been exceedingly valuable to the rebel authorities," so he finally spoke up: "I am the person that you are looking for." The Union general impressed Gilmor. "I was prepossessed from the first in his favor by his blunt, though polite and gentlemanly bearing," he later admitted.[25]

Gilmor told the general that he would have to come with him. "I replied that I was disabled by a wound," explained Franklin, "and could not walk or ride on horseback, and did not think my detention would be legitimate." Gilmor, added the officer, "intimated that his opinion was different, and I left the car with him." Gilmor put Franklin and several other captured officers under guard in the telegraph office at Magnolia Station.[26]

As it turned out, Gilmor knew several women aboard the train, and one of them was ultimately charged and tried before a military tribunal for certain acts that she allegedly committed that day. Gilmor had no idea what offense she was formally charged with, but he would later claim that she was guilty only of being joyous at seeing friendly soldiers take the train. General Franklin personally intervened in the matter.

24 William B. Franklin to Anne Weiser, August 26, 1864, William B. Franklin Papers, Special Collections, Connecticut State Library, Hartford, Connecticut.

25 Gilmor, *Four Years in the Saddle*, 194.

26 Franklin to Weiser, August 26, 1864; Gilmor, *Four Years in the Saddle*, 194.

GEORGE CADWALADER
The major general's large estate lay in the path of Gilmor's raiders.

Library of Congress

In May 1865, he wrote to Gilmor, who was by that time in U.S. custody at Fort McHenry, admitted that the woman "is not guilty of the acts with which she is charged. If not released, I will see to it."[27]

With the engineer missing, Gilmor realized that he had no way to run the train up to Havre de Grace, so he burned the locomotive (named "Henry Clay") instead. A detail rode on to the large estate of Union Maj. Gen. George Cadwalader at Maxwell's Point, a few miles south along the Gunpowder River, to seize fresh horses. The plantation's manager, however, knew of the proximity of the raiders and had evacuated most of Cadwalader's 125 horses. When the cavalry arrived, only about dozen animals remained.[28]

Gilmor, meanwhile, prepared to catch the next train, which had already left Baltimore. He also sent Capt. Henry Brewer with a flag of truce to the drawbridge over the Gunpowder, which was guarded by 200 Union soldiers from Wilmington, Delaware, and the transport *Juniata*, which had

27 Gilmor, *Four Years in the Saddle*, 195.

28 "Rebels at Magnolia on the Philadelphia, Wilmington & Baltimore," *Valley Spirit*, July 13, 1864.

been sent to help guard the bridge. Gilmor's demand was that the garrison surrender. When he learned they had refused because "they were not ready to do so yet," he considered pushing ahead some sharpshooters to send a more sternly crafted message about the seriousness of his demand. It was at that moment when the second train of twelve cars appeared.[29]

Dr. Nathan P. Rice of the 18th New York Infantry was aboard that train. "I felt a little dubious about the safe passage of the train, owing to some stories which were told me in Baltimore," recalled Dr. Rice, "but as no anxiety was manifested by the railroad agent, and as the other train was in advance, I felt assured that we could run through unmolested." His confidence was misplaced. "Just having turned the curve beyond the picket, I noticed that the brakes were suddenly put on."[30]

The Confederate cavalrymen quickly and easily captured the second train, but this engineer also escaped. Gilmor, however, managed to run the train up to Magnolia Station himself, where he unloaded it in the same manner as the first, taking care that each passenger received his or her baggage.[31]

"I at once hid my watch and money, and went out on the platform," continued Doctor Rice. He continued:

> On the road I could see nothing but a train stopped at a station about half a mile ahead. Feeling assured I went back to my seat, replaced my watch and money, when, for the first time, a shot was fired, followed a moment after by a volley. At this time the train had started up, and had

29 Gilmor to Booth, July 28, 1864.

30 "The Magnolia Raid."

31 Gilmor, *Four Years in the Saddle*, 195.

> the engineer reversed his engine, instead of jumping from it, the train might have been saved.[32]

Nellie Noye, a young woman from New York working as a nurse at the Naval Academy Hospital in Annapolis, Maryland, was also aboard the second train. "At the sound of firing I looked out and saw the soldiers by the side of the track. A rebel soldier helped me off the train," she recalled years later. "Our luggage being placed on a handcar, we made our way to the river, where we stayed until morning, and were then taken by steamer to Havre de Grace." Nellie never returned to the field hospital.[33]

A man and a woman approached Gilmor while the train was being unloaded. When Gilmor noticed the woman was distressed, he asked if she had suffered any inconvenience or had been molested in any way. She replied in the negative, but added that she was alone with two or three children and a large quantity of baggage to look after, which she feared losing. Gilmor assured her all would be well. With the assistance of a lieutenant, they unloaded her three large trunks and had them carried to a shady spot under a large tree about 100 yards away, after which she thanked Gilmor profusely.

Much to his disgust, Gilmor soon thereafter came across a lengthy account by the woman in a Northern newspaper in which she claimed she suffered $3,000 in damages at the hands of Gilmor and his "traitorous thieves." Gilmor categorically denied the allegations of wrongdoing.[34]

Gilmor maintained a good head of steam in the locomotive while the train was being unloaded. When everything was

32 "The Rebel Guerrillas," *New York Times*, July 14, 1864.

33 Ellen Oilver Smith, "The Magnolia Station Train Raid." www.madonna.edu/pages/ mmtrain.cfm.

34 Gilmor, *Four Years in the Saddle.*, 195-196.

The burning of the bridge spanning the Gunpowder River.

Pictorial History of the Civil War

clear, he ordered Captain Bayley and his sharpshooters to move up and try to drive the Union infantry from the bridge. The generally ineffective fire wounded one of the Delaware militiamen. Gilmor ran the train up the drawbridge, set it ablaze and "backed the whole flaming mass down on the bridge, catching some of the infantry a little way from shore upon the structure, and compelling them to jump into the water," recalled Gilmor. "The train was running slowly, and stopped right on the draw, where it burned and fell through, communicating the fire and destroying the most important part of the bridge." Bayley reported that some of the green infantry who had jumped into the river to escape the blazing locomotive had swum for the protection of the gunboat. The sight of the burning train left quite an impression on young Nellie Noye. "The appearance of the tilted stack of the engine above the wreck of the bridge is still strong in my memory," she recalled six decades later in 1924.[35]

35 Smith, "The Magnolia Station Train Raid"; *OR* 37, 1:230.

Captain Stirling led the rest of his green Delaware infantrymen to the center of the drawbridge, where they joined Lieutenant Price and his Buckeyes approaching from the southern end of the bridge. "I immediately started for bridge and saw the train just coming on the other end on fire," reported Price. "Upon going near to it I found the captain [Stirling] and his company in advance of the train coming toward me." Working together, the Union soldiers uncoupled two of the train cars and pushed them to safety.

About an hour earlier, reported Price, "the steamer *Juniata* came up the river and anchored 300 yards below the bridge." Something seemed amiss, for "She had no colors hoisted, neither did she communicate with the shore, which caused us to look on her with suspicion." It was not until nearly two hours later that "she hoisted the Stars and Stripes, and at the time the bridge was being fired she steamed up a little nearer, but did not use her gun."[36]

Despite their best efforts, a portion of the bridge was severely damaged, and the burning locomotive fell through the drawbridge and dropped into the river below. The wind blew the flames toward the armed transport, which hastily hoisted anchor and slipped out of harm's way. Gilmor sent a flag of truce to Acting Ensign William J. Herring, in command of the *Juniata*, to let him know his men would not fire on his ship if he steamed to the beach to take the railroad passengers to Havre de Grace. Herring took him up on the offer. Price later admitted he was "undecided for a time whether to stay at my post with my little squad or take passage with the company on steamer, but . . . determined to hold" his position until he received further orders.[37]

36 *OR* 37 1:230.

37 U.S. Army officers were less than impressed by Ensign Herring's performance. On July 11, Lew Wallace sent a telegram to Henry Halleck:

While the *Juniata* was so engaged, Gilmor paroled most of the Union officers because he lacked the mounts to take them away and because many were convalescents from field hospitals. He did, however, retain five, including General Franklin. Gilmor's activities disrupted train service on that stretch of the PW&B, but not as severely as he had hoped. Major General Edward O. C. Ord reported to Grant on July 12: "Railroad bridge at Gunpowder only slightly damaged; can be repaired in three days."[38]

* * *

After spending six or seven hours at Magnolia Station, Gilmor knew it was time to leave. His five convalescent prisoners were placed in carriages so they could keep up with the cavalry. The small column headed for Baltimore, intending to cut cross-country to the York Road and enter the city via Charles Street Avenue or Fall's Road, pass through to Franklin Street, and leave by the Franklin Turnpike. "About one o'clock p.m., the cavalcade started from the station in a southwesterly direction," recalled General Franklin. "I accompanied it in the buggy, another captured officer driving me, and two others on horseback. . . . We crossed Gunpowder

"From information just received the bridge over Gunpowder River is burnt. The gun-boat sent up to protect the bridge had no steam up, and permitted the rebels to run a burning train, which they had captured, upon the draw of the bridge." *OR* 37 2:214.

38 Gilmor, *Four Years in the Saddle.*, 196-197; Ackinclose, *Sabres & Pistols*, 117; OR 37, 2:192-194, 247, and 1:229-230. Captain Stirling was promoted to major of the 7th Delaware Infantry for his gallant efforts to defend the bridge.

Major General William B. Franklin carried off in a buggy.

Frank Leslie's Illustrated Newspaper

Creek five or six miles from the railroad, and had a good view of the burning bridge."[39]

Panicked reports spread across the north. Several newspapers picked up a breathless but inaccurate 6:00 p.m. dispatch from Philadelphia:

> It is now ascertained that two trains were destroyed upon the Philadelphia, Wilmington and Baltimore Railroad. The engineers of both escaped, one, however, being robbed of his money and clothing except shirt and pants. The fireman was shot dead. The mail on the early train was taken from the car before the passengers and divided

39 Franklin to Weiser, August 26, 1864, in Lydia Mintern Post, ed. *Soldiers' Letters, From Camp, Battle-Field and Prison* (New York: Bunch & Huntington, 1865), 4110.

> among the captors. Nothing has been heard of the express car, but of course the thieves did not overlook it.[40]

According to a Baltimore paper, "The 10 o'clock express train from Baltimore also shared the same fate. Conductor Bryson of the express train, was robbed of his watch and money, as also the conduct of the first train. The rebels fired the trains and also the freight house at Magnolia, which was consumed." The paper admitted that "the future intentions of the rebels may be, are, of course, conjecture, but the general impression is that they mean to retreat under cover of darkness. The steam ferry boat *Maryland* is safe, and [Havre de Grace] will be defended by the gunboat *Currituck*, whose guns command the approaches."[41]

The paper was wrong: Gilmor did not wait until after dark. Not long into the march, he encountered a man he knew from Baltimore who warned him that "they were expecting us in Baltimore, had collected a large force of militia, and had barricaded the streets." Anxious to secure his prisoners, Gilmor turned and headed toward his hometown of Towson, seven miles north of Baltimore on the York Road.

The riders were within five or six miles of Towson when they learned a force of Union cavalry was there waiting to intercept them. The force consisted of 75 mounted volunteers under Maj. Edward R. Petherbridge, who had led a battalion of Maryland artillery in 1861. Since Gilmor knew the area so well, and as it would be dark by the time they reached Towson, he believed he could fight them if necessary, but evade the enemy if needed. "I determined to heed no one," explained Gilmor, "but push on till we met the enemy, charge

40 "Rebels at Magnolia on the Philadelphia, Wilmington & Baltimore," *Valley Spirit*, July 13, 1864.

41 "Letter From the Raid," *Worcester Daily Spy*, July 12, 1864.

and fight, and, if we could not whip them, fall back, and go round through the heavy woods about Mine Bank Run."[42]

Once the head of the column was within a mile of Towson, Gilmor selected 10 troopers to ride ahead with him to reconnoiter. Captain Bayley and Lt. William Dorsey were to remain with the main body and come up at a steady pace if they heard any firing. Putting spurs to his mare, Gilmor and his handful of troopers galloped into the town with pistols drawn—but all was quiet. No one was expecting him. Some of the local ladies greeted Gilmor as a conquering hero come home.[43]

The major dismounted, drank a glass of ale at Ady's Hotel, and met several acquaintances who begged him to press on. Some were just back from Baltimore and had seen a large force of cavalry riding hard to cut him off. One told Gilmor that at least 1,000 Union horsemen were coming from Baltimore, seven miles distant, and urged him not to delay. Gilmor, however, determined to have at least a brush with the advance guard, declined to leave.[44]

By this time the main body of Gilmor's command arrived in Towson and Bayley formed the men in the square. Pickets were deployed to give timely warning. It did not take long. Soon thereafter, a report arrived that enemy cavalry in considerable force was coming up the turnpike. Gilmor instructed the picket to let the enemy cavalry advance, challenge, fire, and retreat. He personally selected the 10 most reliable men to guard the prisoners and left them under command of his quartermaster, Capt. Nicholas W. Owings, who knew the area well. Gilmor told Owings which roads to take and where to wait for Gilmor should a fast escape be

42 Gilmor, *Four Years in the Saddle*, 197.

43 *Baltimore American*, July 13, 1864.

44 Gilmor, *Four Years in the Saddle*, 198.

necessary. If he did not join him there by daylight, he instructed, Owings and the prisoners were to push on and try to reach Jubal Early's army near Washington.[45]

Gilmor also directed Lt. William H. Kemp to take 15 men and charge the enemy's advance guard, run them back on their main body, and not permit them, in turn, to charge him. Kemp should then retreat with his men to either side of the road to make way for Gilmor and the rest of his command.

News of the approach of a large force of enemy cavalry made some of the Rebels nervous, particularly since they were exhausted after their long high-stakes ride. Few of them knew where they were, but all of appreciated that they were sitting in pitch dark far from any support. Gilmor overhead some of the men say, "I expect the band will go up tonight; but we must stick by [Gilmor]." Another responded, "No fear; he'll take us through all right; only stay by him, and there's no danger." Most of the men understood they faced serious business that night, but none there was nary a word about holding back or shirking duty.[46]

Lieutenant Kemp's party advanced with pistols drawn while the main body drew sabers. Each man settled himself in the saddle to prepare for combat. Gilmor heard the pickets firing on the advance elements of the Federal cavalry. Enemy fire rang in response. Kemp dashed on with a Rebel yell, prompting Gilmor to tell his command to join in with their own Rebel yell and to keep it up with a will.

The main body moved out at a steady trot. Moments later Kemp and his men rode into the lead Union troopers and apparently drove them back. Gilmor and the main body pressed on. Eventually, the riders at the head made out enemy horsemen approaching in the darkness, trotting down

45 Ibid.

46 Ibid., 198-199.

the middle of the road. When Gilmor recognized Kemp's voice he called off his men. "A good many shots were fired but nobody hurt," a witness recounted.[47]

As it turned out, the Union troopers were mounted on fresh horses and easily outran the weary mounts of the Maryland men, who never got within a saber's reach of them. The Confederates drew their pistols and gave chase, firing at them at the crest of every rolling hill. Gilmor and company chased the Federals for nearly four miles before they broke off the effort. "That night a number of recruits from the city joined my command, and we were told by them that the whole picket-line on that side of Baltimore was broken," recorded Gilmor, "and that the cavalry had not stopped running until they reached the Bel Air market in the city."[48]

Satisfied with the evening's work, Gilmor and his troopers returned to Towson with only one wounded. Anxious to rejoin Owings, who had continued on some way ahead, Gilmor pushed on with his entire command. The exhaustion was simply too much for many to bear, and some were snoring in their saddles before they had even marched a mile. To prevent any of them from getting lost Gilmor decided to ride in the rear of the column. Some of his troopers toppled from the saddle and would not wake until shaken or roughly dragged along the road. Exhaustion caught up with Gilmor, who also fell asleep in the saddle. Somehow he had left the road and was swaying on his horse when a loud voice roused him from his slumber:

"Halt!"

His mount stopped, throwing Gilmor against its neck, The same voice yelled again:

47 Ibid., 199-200; Joseph Judge, *Season of Fire: The Confederate Strike on Washington* (Charlottesville, VA: Rockbridge Press, 1994), 242.

48 Gilmor, *Four Years in the Saddle*, 202.

"Halt!"

Something was clearly amiss. Gilmor replied, "A friend."

"Friend to whom?"

"To the Union," lied Gilmor, "I belong to the 1st Virginia Cavalry, and my company has been out in Harford County, on a scout after Gilmor's raiders. My captain sent me ahead to tell you he was coming, so that you would not fire on him."

"All right," replied the gullible picket.

"I'll go back and tell him to come on," added the quick-thinking Gilmor.

The officer later admitted he was so tired that he was almost hallucinating and did not know where he was, but while talking to the picket thought he could make out the railroad track in the distance. He concluded he was near the Relay House on the Northern Central Railroad.

After riding about 100 yards, Gilmor struck out across the fields and reached the crossing of the road to Towson from which he had strayed while asleep. He found one of his men there fast asleep, left in the column's wake by Captain Bayley to wait for the wandering Gilmor. The colonel woke the man and learned the rest of the command had crossed the road safely and were waiting for him at a nearby meetinghouse. Gilmor found them there lying along the road, scattered about and sleeping soundly. "Had I been captured they would have slept till morning," he concluded, "and no doubt many of them would have joined me, and we should have been a pleasant little party for Fort McHenry."[49]

Gilmor roused his men and soon had them moving once again through the pitch-dark night. They passed through Green Spring Valley until they reached the farm where he had told Owings to wait for him. The detachment of guards were asleep in the road and the carriage in which Franklin

49 Ibid., 201.

A woodcut depiction of the nighttime escape of Major General Franklin from his guards near Towson.

Frank Leslie's Illustrated Newspaper

had been riding sat empty. Gilmor turned to Capt. James L. Clark: "I'll bet Franklin is gone."

The two officers rode through the guard detachment twice without waking a man. Gilmor dismounted, roused them, and asked for Franklin. One guard replied that the Union general was "in the fence corner with the other prisoners." In fact, no one was there.[50]

"Right glad I am that my pious friends were not there to hear me when I found that Franklin had indeed escaped," declared Gilmor. "I fear they would have considered me somewhat ruffled."

They searched in vain for the disabled general, but he was no where to be found. "It will be readily seen that I had a very valued companion in the person of the general, and I could

50 Gilmor, Four Years in the Saddle, 202.

Maj. Gen. Franklin hiding in the woods to avoid scouts.

Frank Leslie's Illustrated Newspaper

not fail, under the circumstances, to appreciate his society very highly," continued Gilmor, "so, as I say, being greatly provoked when I found that he had ceased to honor us with his presence, I swore with unusual energy. By this means my men were as effectually roused as if a broadside had been opened upon them."[51]

What had transpired was no mystery. When his escort decided to stop, Owings told Franklin to bed down in a fence corner. Soon enough, all of his captors were sound asleep. "I now saw that the opportunity for which I had been anxiously waiting ever since my capture had arrived," recalled Franklin,

51 Ibid., 201-202.

Maj. Gen. Franklin's reception by Maryland farmers.

Frank Leslie's Illustrated Newspaper

"and with a fervent prayer for strength, I resolved to attempt an escape."[52]

After making sure the guards really were truly asleep by coughing and yawning loudly, Franklin rose and deliberately but quietly made his way through the sleeping men, determined to get as far as his wounded leg would take him. He made his way through some dense woods, across an open field, and into another stand of trees until he found himself on the edge of a cultivated valley. He was thoroughly exhausted by the time dawn arrived, and crawled into a thicket of blackberry bushes to wait until the next sunset. Somehow he had made it about two miles on his gimpy leg.

52 Lydia Mintern, Post, ed. *Soldiers' Letters, From Camp, Battle-Field and Prison* (New York: Bunch & Huntington, 1865), 412.

"In my weak state," he recalled, "annoyed by the sun and mosquitoes, I passed an exceedingly uncomfortable day."[53]

Gilmor allowed his weary command to eat and feed and groom their horses before going out to search for Franklin. He admitted agonizing over the thought of being blamed for the careless manner in which Franklin had been allowed to escape. When the searched turned up no trace of the former prisoner, Gilmor allowed his troopers to get a few hours of additional rest. Gilmor changed clothes in a nearby house and spent a few minutes examining the contents of Franklin's suitcase, in which he found a prayer book presented by his sister, some photographs, and a silver snuff box inlaid with gold. He made arrangements to have the valise returned to its owner.[54]

By the time darkness arrived Franklin was hallucinating from pain, hunger, and exhaustion. He set out across the valley, and even though it was only about a mile wide, the journey took him an hour to traverse. The famished and weak officer found only a few cabbage leaves to eat in the garden of a farmer. "I had become so exhausted that I was determined to get something to eat on the next morning either from friend or foe," he admitted, having reached his breaking point. By the time of the next sunrise he moved toward a small house. Franklin convinced two nearby farmers he came upon to take him to the owner of the house. Fortunately for the general, the owner was a Union man who happily fed him before sending word to Baltimore that he had an important guest at his table.[55]

At 1:00 a.m. on July 14, a detachment of the 8th Illinois Cavalry arrived to escort Franklin back to Baltimore. "I was

53 Franklin to Weiser, August 26, 1864.

54 Gilmor, *Four Years in the Saddle*, 202-203.

55 Franklin to Weiser, August 26, 1864.

once more within our lines in the hands of friends," wrote a grateful Franklin, "thankful I had for this time escaped the horrors of a rebel prison."[56]

* * *

While Franklin was undergoing his ordeal, Harry Gilmor and his command were spending the the day near Pikesville, just northwest of the Baltimore city limits. The colonel, with about sixty of his men, rode to Rose Hill, an estate in Pikesville where they spent a pleasant evening in the company of many of the young ladies. While Gilmor was enjoying the hospitality of Rose Hill, a detachment of cavalry and Union League volunteers made a half-hearted sortie out of the defenses of Baltimore; a detachment led by Sgt. Alonzo Travers of Co. A of the 2nd Maryland quickly chased them back.[57]

Gilmor intended to burn the U. S. Arsenal in Pikesville and sent a detachment under Capt. James L. Clark of Co. F, 2nd Maryland Cavalry, to do so. Gilmor's uncle, Benjamin C. Howard, lived a mile west of the town of Pikesville and was there that morning when the raiders arrived. Howard sought out Captain Clark and pleaded with the cavalryman not to destroy the arsenal because the destruction would only serve to hurt the town and its residents—and probably bring retribution by the Federal government upon the town, some of whom's residents were loyal to the Southern cause.

56 Abner N. Hard, *History of the Eighth Cavalry Regiment Illinois Volunteers, During the Great Rebellion* (Aurora, IL: privately published, 1868), 302; Franklin to Weiser, August 26, 1864.

57 Erick F. Davis, ed., "A Pikesville Diary of 1864," *History Trails*, Vol. 13, No. 3 (Spring 1979), 11-12.

Howard's logic prevailed and Clark spared the arsenal complex.[58]

That afternoon, a force of Union infantry that included Companies B, E, G, and I of the 159th Ohio Infantry, together with some other troops, marched on Pikesville with the hope of attacking and bagging the illusive Gilmor. Captain Clark and his detachment, however, were long gone by the time the Buckeyes finally arrived.[59]

Gilmor sent a sergeant and 10 men to within four miles of Baltimore and rode himself to the Seven-mile House on the Reisterstown Road, where he soon dropped off to sleep. Gilmor spent the night there, and felt fully refreshed when reveille sounded the next morning. The Rebel column moved out at sunrise, with Captain Owings leading the way since he knew the country well. The troopers headed toward Rockville, where Gilmor expected to join General Early and his army. Evening was approaching when word arrived that Early had retreated to Poolesville, and that the enemy had possession of Rockville. The riders changed course and rode all night through Montgomery County for Poolesville.[60]

Gilmor and his men reached Bradley Johnson's headquarters about two miles below Poolesville at daybreak. "He was delighted to see me safely back, saying that when he left me near Baltimore, he felt certain I should be captured," recounted Gilmor. "I felt very well pleased myself to be where I was, having made, without doubt, a rather venturesome trip."

After breakfast and some skirmishing, Gilmor reported to Early's headquarters. Generals Early and John C.

58 Ibid., 12.

59 Whitelaw Reid, *Ohio in the War: Her Statesmen, Generals, and Soldiers*, 2 vols. (Cincinnati: The Robert Clarke Co., 1895), 2:689.

60 Gilmor, *Four Years in the Saddle*, 203.

Breckinridge greeted the colonel warmly and told him that they had given him up for lost. "They complimented me highly for the success of the expedition, and regretted the escape of General Franklin." Gilmor dined with the two generals and spent the day at headquarters. "When I told General Early with what ease I could have captured Baltimore with a few more men, he regretted heartily that a brigade could not have been given me, and he did me the honor to say I had deserved promotion; and I should have had his recommendation, I feel sure, whenever I had applied to him."[61]

Gilmor had every reason to brag about the performance of his command. "During the whole time and under the most trying circumstances both men & officers behaved with coolness, skill and courage," he declared in his report of the raid, "and though they suffered very much from loss of sleep & could scarcely sit on their horses they were always obedient." He reported seven men lost: Sergeant Field killed, and "probably 6 men captured while straggling."[62]

Gilmor's timing was fortunate. Once he learned of General Franklin's plight, Lt. Gen. Ulysses S. Grant told Assistant Secretary of War Charles A. Dana, "Boldness is all that is wanted to [drive the] enemy out of Maryland in confusion." The end of the raid came just in time: Grant was preparing to muster all available forces to drive Early's pesky army away, once and for all.[63]

Harry Gilmor's adventure was over, and with it ended the desperate and yet little-known Johnson-Gilmor Raid.

61 Ibid., 204.

62 Gilmor to Booth, July 28, 1864. Gilmor returned with just one wounded from the fight near Towson on July 12. The wound was apparently not significant enough to include it in the report.

63 John Y. Simon, ed., *The Papers of Ulysses S. Grant*, 32 vols. (Carbondale: Southern Illinois University Press, 1967-2012), 11:228.

CONCLUSION

AFTER CROSSING the Potomac River to safety, Jubal Early and his plucky little army fell back to the vicinity of Winchester, Virginia.

He launched a cavalry raid into Pennsylvania at the end of July under Brig. Gen. John McCausland that culminated with the burning of the town of Chambersburg in retaliation for Maj. Gen. David Hunter's burning of homes and towns in Virginia. Colonel William E. Peters of the 21st Virginia refused to obey the order to torch the town and McCausland had him arrested. Most of the town burned to the ground, meaning that the level of cruelty in an already cruel war had stepped up a notch. Early withdrew his command to Winchester and waited for the Union to come and get him. For the time being, the war in the northern reaches of the Shenandoah Valley had stalled. All of that changed in mid-September. A lot happened before that time.[1]

Early's strike on Washington cleared the Valley of Union troops for most of the summer of 1864. This, in turn, allowed

1 John Y. Simon, ed., *The Papers of Ulysses S. Grant*, 32 vols. (Carbondale: Southern Illinois University Press, 1967-2012), 11:228.

crops to be grown in the Breadbasket of the Confederacy. Lee's "Bad Old Man" won a battle at Monocacy that he had never intended to fight. The success slowed his approach to Fort Stevens, which was now well-defended by veteran Union troops. Early's drive north had drawn two infantry corps, the VI and XIX, away from the siege lines at Petersburg, both of which reinforced the capital. Grant was left to face Lee with a much smaller command than he desired.

Grant relieved General Hunter when he refused to surrender field command and turned it over to the commander of the Army of the Potomac's Cavalry Corps, 33-year-old Maj. Gen. Philip H. Sheridan. The plucky horseman would take control of the Union forces gathering to go after Early and his Valley army, including the Union VIII Corps.

Sheridan assumed command on August 8, 1864. Five weeks later he kicked off a campaign that inflicted four sharp battlefield defeats on his opponent. Early's strike on Washington and subsequent retreat into the Valley may have bought the Confederacy several months of additional life.[2]

* * *

The Johnson-Gilmor Raid, which was a sideshow of the strike on Washington, had no real chance of succeeding. The two-day delay in delivering the operational orders to Bradley T. Johnson doomed the cavalry raid to failure. Even without that two days, the timetable for the expedition was wholly unrealistic, and Johnson from the outset understood that it could not succeed. Still, he did his best he could under difficult circumstances. Johnson later offered a concise

2 For one of the best overviews of the 1864 Valley Campaign, see Jeffry D. Wert, *From Winchester to Cedar Creek: The Shenandoah Campaign of 1864* (Carlisle, PA: South Mountain Press, 1987).

explanation for why the combined arms portion of the raid did not materialize:

> The co-operative movement on Point Lookout failed, I have since understood, because the secret expedition of John Taylor Wood, by sea from Wilmington, was spoken of on the streets of Richmond, the day before he was to have started from Wilmington. It was, therefore, countermanded, because the Confederate authorities well knew that the Federal general was so well served that he was accurately and promptly informed of everything as soon as it transpired in Richmond.[3]

Early's division commander, Maj. Gen. John B. Gordon, also blamed Grant's swift response to Early's threatening of Washington for the failure of the raid. After Early decided to withdraw after the skirmish at Fort Stevens: "Our . . . retreat from [Washington was] so necessary to avoid being captured ourselves by the heavy forces just arriving from Grant's army, cooperating with those forming in our rear, the recruiting of our ranks by releasing our expectant boys at Point Lookout had to be abandoned. There was not enough time for the delicate and difficult task of communicating secretly with our prisoner so as to have them ready for prompt cooperation in overpowering the negro guards," Gordon continued, "nor time for procuring the flotillas necessary silently to transport across the Potomac the forces who were to assault the fortress."[4]

Harry Gilmor, who played such an important role in the unfolding of these events, later reported that Robert E. Lee had declared "that the cutting of the Philadelphia road was the only part of the programme in the Maryland campaign

3 For the best overview of the 1864 Valley Campaign, see Jeffry D. Wert, *From Winchester to Cedar Creek: The Shenandoah Campaign of 1864* (Carlisle, PA: South Mountain Press, 1987).

4 Gordon, *Reminiscences*, 316.

that was carried out successfully." That declaration, declared Gilmor, "was reward enough for the part I had borne in it."[5] As pointed out in Chapter 6, the drawbridge over the Gunpowder River was back in service just a few days after Gilmor burned it; the strategic significance of the Magnolia Station raid was minimal, at best.

Despite the early termination of the raid without fulfilling its mission, the men of Johnson's mounted brigade remained proud of their part in the operation. For those involved in the raid, explained one veteran, "It was one of the greatest feats of the war, and should be written as it was on the bright pages of the history of the War Between the States."[6]

The bold and well-executed cavalry raids drew resources away from Early's front and disrupted communications and logistics in and out of the national capital and Baltimore. With a more realistic schedule and the waterborne arm of the operation, the Point Lookout portion of the raid might have had some chance of success; history, however, demonstrates that the odds of pulling it off were low, indeed.

The failure of the Johnson-Gilmor Raid meant that the suffering of the prisoners of war continued. Only the end of the war liberated the survivors. Once Gen. Joseph E. Johnston capitulated at Bennett Place on April 26, 1865, the prisoners there finally began to recognize that the Confederacy was no more. It was not until June 12 that news arrived that if the prisoners took the oath of loyalty to the United States, they would be released and permitted to go home to their families. Some 500 to 600 men took the oath per day and were freed. Camp Hoffman finally shut down on August 2, 1865. Within a year, all of the public property on Point Lookout had been sold, and, other than the large

5 Gilmor, *Four Years in the Saddle*, 204-205.

6 Ibid.

Confederate cemetery there, any trace of either the Hammond General Hospital or Camp Hoffman disappeared. More than 52,000 Confederate prisoners passed through its gates during the term of its existence.

As noted, some 4,000 Confederate prisoners never made it home. Most remain at Point Lookout in a two-acre cemetery purchased by the government of Maryland. The cemetery, which was eventually turned over to the Federal government, was dedicated as part of the Centennial of the United States on July 4, 1876. The dead bear silent witness to the suffering of those unfortunate enough to occupy Camp Hoffman.[7]

7 Bradley M. Gottfried and Linda I. Gottfried, *Hell Comes of Southern Maryland: The Story of Point Lookout Prison and Hammond General Hospital* (Fairfield, PA: Turning Point Publishing, 2018), 104-109.

Appendix A

Confederate Order of Battle

Army of the Valley
Lt. Gen. Jubal A. Early

Cavalry Division
Maj. Gen. Robert Ransom

Johnson's Brigade
Brig. Gen. Bradley T. Johnson

1st Maryland Cavalry (Capt. Warner Welsh)
2nd Maryland Cavalry (Lt. Col. Harry Gilmor)
8th Virginia Cavalry (Col. James M. Corns)
21st Virginia Cavalry (Col. William E. Peters)
34th Battalion of Virginia Cavalry (Lt. Col. Vincent Witcher)
36th Battalion of Virginia Cavalry (Maj. James M. Sweeney)
37th Battalion of Virginia Cavalry (Lt. Col. Ambrose C. Dunn)
2nd Maryland Light Artillery (Baltimore Light Artillery)
(Lt. John R. McNulty)

Appendix B

Cavalry Raids

As a general statement, cavalry raids during the Civil War had limited effectiveness, and the Johnson-Gilmor Raid was no exception.

The raid's hasty and unrealistic schedule was saddled with miserable operational security that eventually led to the seaborne part of the plan being scrubbed from the start. As noted earlier, and as an original title of this book once explicitly stated, the Johnson-Gilmor Raid was "destined to fail." At the same time, the desire to free prisoners of war from their suffering is a powerful one. The Johnson-Gilmor Raid was one of three such documented instances during 1864 alone.

Chronologically, the first was the failed Kilpatrick- Dahlgren Raid of February-March 1864, which was briefly described in Chapter One.

The second was the Johnson-Gilmor Raid, which was aborted before it ever really got started.

At the end of July 1864, a third attempt was launched by Maj. Gen. William T. Sherman. Maj. Gen. George Stoneman, the former commander of the Army of the Potomac's Cavalry Corps, was in Georgia and by the summer of 1864 was in command of a division of cavalry assigned to the Army of Ohio.

Stoneman's mission was about to destroy Gen. John B. Hood's lines of communication and supply between Macon and Atlanta. Just as he was ready to begin, explained Sherman, the cavalier handed his superior "a letter asking permission, after fulfilling his orders and breaking the road, to be allowed, with his command

GEORGE STONEMAN
The major general was captured leading a raid in the summer of 1864 to free Union prisoners of war held at Andersonville.

Library of Congress

proper, to proceed to Macon and Andersonville and release our prisoners of war confined at those points." Sherman was sympathetic to the plight of the unfortunate prisoners. "There was something most captivating in the idea," he later admitted, "and the execution was within the bounds of probable success." Sherman gave his consent. "[If you can bring back to the army any or all of those prisoners of war, it will be an achievement that will entitle you, and your command, to the love and admiration of the whole country."

Stoneman's plan not only failed to free a single captive, but was an abject disaster. Southern cavalry fought him on July 30 at Dunlap's Farm, and cornered his horsemen at the Battle of Sunshine Church on the 31st, compelling him to surrender a large portion of his command. The general, to his great humiliation, ended up a prisoner of war at Macon.[1]

Gen. George S. Patton, Jr. fell into a similar trap during World War II. In March of 1945, as the war was winding down, Patton ordered the 4th Armored Division to form a task force to free the American prisoners of war being held at a camp in Hammelburg, Germany. About 10,000 men, including 1,500 American officers, were kept there, including Patton's son-in-law Lt. Col. John K.

1 *OR* 38, 5:264, 265. For a monograph on this failed raid, see Byron H. Mathews, Jr., *The McCook-Stoneman Raid* (Philadelphia: Dorrance & Co., 1976).

GEORGE S. PATTON, JR.
Few people know that the famous World War II commander ordered a task force to free American prisoners of war—one of whom was Patton's own son-in-law.

National Portrait Gallery

Waters, who was captured at the 1943 Battle of Kasserine Pass in North Africa. Capt. Abraham J. Baum led the expedition.

On March 26, Lt. Col. Creighton Abrams, commanding officer of Combat Command B, 4th Armored Division, assigned one company of Sherman medium tanks and one platoon of M5A1 Stuart light tanks, one company of armored infantry, a reconnaissance platoon, and a motorized assault gun platoon to form Task Force Baum, which consisted of 314 soldiers and 57 vehicles.

That evening (March 26) the task force moved out but quickly met with heavy opposition and immediately fell behind schedule. Task Force Baum continued on and arrived at the prisoner of war camp the next day. The Americans mistook Serbian prisoners of war clad in gray uniforms for German soldiers and opened fire. Waters volunteered to exit the camp

ABRAHAM BAUM
The captain was tasked by Patton to command Task Force Baum.

National Museum of Jewish American Military History

JOHN K. WATERS
George Patton's son-in-law was a colonel when held as a POW, and is shown here as a general.

USAHEC

to notify the Americans of the mistake, but a German soldier shot and severely wounded him.

Baum quickly realized there were too many men for his small command to liberate. After a short rest, he tried to withdraw but without the wounded Waters, who was taken to the camp hospital because he was too injured to be removed safely. The delays allowed the Germans to cobble together an effective defense.

The Americans failed when they tried to cut their way out on the morning of March 28, forcing Baum to order "every man for himself." The effort was a complete disaster, a more modern echo of the failed Stoneman Raid. Baum was wounded and captured. Of the 314 officers and men, 26 were killed and most of the rest captured by the Germans. All 57 of the task force's vehicles were destroyed or captured. Just 10 days later, the entire camp, including the wounded Waters, was liberated.[2]

Armor is the modern equivalent of cavalry and often uses similar tactics. In fact, armored units are sometimes designated as cavalry and often carries out the same duty previously performed by mounted cavalrymen. Indeed, Patton himself was an old horseman, so it was probably appropriate for him to carry on with the tradition of cavalry attempting to liberate prisoners of war. It would have

2 For a detailed look at the actions of Task Force Baum, see Richard Baron, Abe Baum, and Richard Goldhurst, *Raid! The Untold Story of Patton's Secret Mission* (New York: Random House, 1981).

made complete sense to him. Unfortunately, Patton failed to learn the right lesson from the three failed attempts during the American Civil War, and his own attempt in 1945 failed just as miserably.

* * *

The Johnson-Gilmor Raid was the brainchild of Robert E. Lee, often considered one of the greatest military minds in American history. William T. Sherman, also considered to be one of the great captains of American history and one of pantheon of greats that led the Union to victory in the Civil War, specifically approved the Stoneman Raid. George Patton, one of the finest American battlefield commander of the Twentieth Century, cooked up the hare-brained scheme that led to debacle that befell Task Force Baum.

Three of the greatest commanders in the history of the United States fell victim to the siren song of attempting to free prisoners of war. All failed, proving that even great generals are capable of making terrible decisions. Why? Because they are human beings with empathy who tried to alleviate the suffering of their comrades being held prisoner. The sentiment is understandable and commendable, but it demonstrates that even great commanders fail to learn the lessons of history.

Basic logistics notwithstanding—and make no mistake, transporting, arming, and feeding a large body of freed prisoners of war was a daunting task at best—even if the prisoners could be liberated and transported, they were sick, malnourished, and in poor physical condition. The likelihood of their being able to perform service of any value was slim at best, and to expect them to return to combat duty in the near future was not reasonable or realistic.

The Johnson-Gilmor Raid reflects the desperation and stress weighing upon General Lee to make good the losses sustained by his Army of Northern Virginia as a consequence of Ulysses S. Grant's grinding war of attrition. Once the prisoner exchange cartel ended, replacing lost soldiers became all that more challenging for the Confederacy. Its deficit in manpower was lopsided at the beginning of the war, and by the summer of 1864 it was stretched to its limits. It was unreasonable to expect freed prisoners of war to be in any condition to make a difference without a significant period of time for recuperation, which in itself was not a viable option.

As a result, the daring Johnson-Gilmor Raid was destined from the outset to fail.

Appendix C

Caring for Cavalry Horses While on a Raid

RAIDS "are seldom worth their cost in horse flesh, and the damage done to the cavalry to the detriment of the raiders," declared Capt. Alonzo Gray of the 14th U.S. Cavalry in his 1910 analysis of the role of horse soldiers in the Civil War. "The results of a raid will necessarily be temporary, and the damage done soon repaired; and as stated by [Lt. Gen. Ulysses S.] Grant, they 'contribute very little to the grand result'."[1] Although most Civil War raids failed, though could still have strategic significance.

In the case of Confederate cavalry, the Southerners typically rode their own horses they had brought with them from home rather than government-issued mounts and used their own tack and saddles. If a Confederate cavalryman lost his horse, he often had to return to his home to find a replacement if one could not be found in the field, meaning that his regiment would be deprived of his services while on leave to find a remount. If a remount could not be located, the soldier would often be transferred to the infantry or artillery, meaning that Southern cavalry regiments were normally

1 Alonzo Gray, *Cavalry Tactics as Illustrated by the War of the Rebellion, Together with May Interesting Facts Important for Cavalry to Know* (Fort Leavenworth, KS: U.S. Cavalry Assoc., 1910), 138-139.

undersized and often indifferently mounted. A lengthy cavalry raid could therefore wreak havoc on a cavalry command.

The rate of march for cavalry operating in the field—usually riding in a column of four across—was governed by circumstances like the state of the animals involved, the condition of the roads, prevailing weather conditions, and the object of the march. The desired rate of march was typically five miles per hour, alternating between the walk (four miles per hour) and the trot (six and a half miles per hour). Troopers dismounted periodically, particularly when ascending or descending steep hills. The average daily march for veteran cavalry was about twenty-five miles per day, with regular halts for water and rest. In emergencies cavalry could cover fifty miles in twenty-four hours, and if a single march as much as one hundred miles during the same time-frame.

Of course, the ability to cover such distances depended on the circumstances noted above. "Without proper preparation a command will not be able to make such marches, either campaign or forced, and to accomplish such marches will be impossible unless the horses are in condition for it, and an attempt to do so would merely result in the destruction of a cavalry command through disabling or killing the horses," correctly noted Lt. John J. Boniface of the 4th U.S. Cavalry in 1903.

"It is best to change the order of marching so that the troops in rear of the column on one day march at the head of the column on the next, and so on," wrote cavalryman Boniface. "It is extremely fatiguing to march in the rear of a column of cavalry, where the dust is always thick and the gait more or less irregular, and the change from the rear to the head of a column should also be made within the troop itself by changing the platoons from day to day." Finding oneself at the rear of a column of cavalry was indeed the most miserable place. The dust was thick and choking there, the smell of sweat and horse excrement permeated the air, and horse flies buzzed about in heavy number, making man and beast alike miserable.[2]

Despite their size and strength, horses are fragile. They require rest, fodder, fresh water, and personal care and attention in order to keep them in decent physical condition. "The horse is the most important care of the cavalry soldier," stated an 1864 field manual for Union cavalrymen. "No one is fit to be in the mounted service who will not look after the welfare of his horse with more solicitude than he does after his own." There was a great deal of work involved in keeping horses healthy, much of which was not possible during a raid, where speed and constant motion were usually required.

The daily allowance for horses was at least four gallons of clean water per day—if you could find it and if the animal would drink when it was available. Horses were supposed to be groomed daily. Their hooves and shoes required daily attention; a lame horse cannot march very far. They were to be fed three times per day, preferably with grain rather than grass or clover because the latter, while filling, is not particularly nutritious. Each of these activities takes time, which is normally a rare commodity for a cavalry column on a raid, where constant speedy movement is essential. Consequently, horses regularly failed during lengthy cavalry raids, either breaking down and being left by the side of the road to be nursed back to health, or they collapsed and died, leaving their riders to make their way along on foot, left to their own devices to find a replacement mount.[3]

By the time of the Johnson-Gilmor Raid in the summer of 1864, Confederate cavalrymen were veteran horse soldiers who understood the need to care for their horses and the implications of losing one. If a mount broke down on a raid into enemy territory and could not be replaced, its rider would end up walking behind the

2 John J. Boniface, *The Cavalry Horse and His Pack, Embracing the Practical Details of Cavalry Service* (Kansas City, MO: Hudson-Kimberly Pub. Co., 1903), 224-226.

3 James A. Congdon, *Congdon's Cavalry Compendium: Containing Instructions for Non-Commissioned Officers and Privates in the Cavalry Service* (Philadelphia: J. B. Lippincott, 1864), 23, 24-28.

column carrying his saddle and likely be snapped up as a prisoner of war. Robert E. Lee's plan was audacious. Veterans or not, the risks of the Johnson-Gilmor raid were high and probably outweighed any perceived reward.

Appendix D

The Strange Case of Henry Onderdonk

WHEN BRADLEY T. Johnson's Confederate raiders visited the campus of the Maryland Agricultural College on July 12, 1864, Henry Onderdonk, the college's president, warmly welcomed them and arranged for the Southern troopers to be fed by the college's kitchen staff.

Why would an esteemed college president from New York working in a border state during a civil war risk his entire career to help Confederate raiders? That intriguing question triggered a federal investigation. The answer to that important question remains a mystery to this day.

Henry Onderdonk was a member of the Knickerbockers, one of the original Dutch families to settle Manhattan. He was born in New York City on June 15, 1822, the son of William Onderdonk, the brother of the Right Reverend Benjamin T. Onderdonk, and the Right Reverend Henry U. Onderdonk—the Episcopal bishops of New York and Pennsylvania. Henry was educated at Columbia College (now Columbia University), where he earned his master of arts degree and later attended a seminary for about a year, although he did not complete that program.

After graduation, Onderdonk relocated to St. Timothy's Hall, a small military academy located in Catonsville, Maryland, where he taught school. Subsequently, he taught at Govansville and Green Spring Valley. In 1861, he was elected as president of the Maryland Agricultural College (today known as the University of Maryland),

HENRY U. ONDERDONK

The president of Maryland Agricultural College in 1864.

Archives, St. James College

the first agricultural research college established in the United States. He was "well known in educational circles as an able, conservative teacher," as one obituary noted in 1895.[1]

The college was chartered on March 6, 1856. In 1858, the trustees issued stock to help launch the institution, and for a purchase price of $20,000, they chose 428 acres of Charles Benedict Calvert's Riversdale Farm in present-day College Park in Prince George's County as the site for the college.[2]

The institution was formally dedicated on October 5, 1859, with Joseph Henry, the head of the Smithsonian Institution, as the keynote speaker at the dedication ceremony. Thirty-four students, including the four sons of Charles Benedict Calvert, George, Charles, William, and Eugene, enrolled in the initial class. Benjamin Hallowell served as president for one month after the opening of the college. John Work Scott was elected president of the college in 1860, but never arrived on campus. John M. Colby served as president from 1860-1861, remaining until Onderdonk was elected and took office.[3]

In July 1862, the same month that the Maryland Agricultural College awarded its first degrees, President Abraham Lincoln signed the Morrill Land Grant Act, which provided federal funds to schools that taught agriculture or engineering, or which provided military training. The college promptly took advantage of this opportunity and officially became a land grant college in February 1864 after the

1 "Mr. Henry Onderdonk. His Funeral and Sketch of His Career as an Educator," *Baltimore Sun*, August 19, 1895; "Henry Onderdonk." *Herald and Torch Light*, August 22, 1895.

2 Charles Benedict Calvert was an important figure in Maryland history. In addition to serving several terms in the state legislature and a single term in Congress (1861-1863), he was an early supporter of the inventors of the telegraph, and he founded the Maryland Agricultural College. He was a direct descendant of the Lords Baltimore, the proprietary governors of the Province of Maryland from 1631-1776. Calvert inherited the family's historic homestead, called Riversdale. He innovated numerous ideas about scientific agriculture, adopted ideas published in various newspapers and journals, and invented a number of innovations. "Respect to the Memory of the Late Hon. Charles B. Calvert," *Daily National Republican*, May 18, 1864.

3 "Timeline: University of Maryland," www.umd.edu/history-and-mission/timeline.

Maryland legislature voted to approve the Morrill Act, all of which occurred during Onderdonk's tenure as president.[4] In April 1864, Maj. Gen. Ambrose E. Burnside and his IX Corps camped on the grounds of the college on their way from Annapolis to Washington, DC. Burnside and his troops were on their way to join the Army of the Potomac for the coming campaign season that became known as the Overland Campaign.[5]

The visit of Johnson and his troopers raised immediate suspicions, particularly since Onderdonk was known to be a strong Southern sympathizer. Several newspapers published unsigned insinuations alleging treason on Onderdonk's part. He replied in print, denying that he was even present that day, claiming, "The only truth in the whole thing is that General Johnson's 'band of raiders' passed through the college grounds. I am mentioned by name as having invited them. I did not invite them...and if they had the 'delicacies of the season,' they must have brought them with them."[6]

William H. Purnell, a member of the college's board of trustees, requested a speedy inquiry by federal authorities to determine the truth of these allegations, so that any guilty parties could be dismissed before the next school term began. Investigators questioned faculty, staff, and other witnesses, sometimes pitting them against each other. No evidence emerged to suggest that there had been anything unplanned about the visit of the Confederate cavalry to the college campus.[7]

John A. Bingham, a powerful Radical Republican Congressman from Ohio, had been commissioned as a major and judge advocate general in the Union Army by his fellow Ohioan and Radical Republican, Secretary of War Edwin M. Stanton. Bingham "issued a precipe by order of the President for the immediate arrest of

4 Ibid.

5 Ibid.

6 For more information, see "Henry Onderdonk," https://www.flickr.com/photos/digitalcollectionum/6258589333.

7 Ibid.

Onderdonk," according to an obscure file found in the National Archives and Records Administration.

An August 1, 1864 notation on the back of the memorandum in the file inquired whether "the warrant for the arrest of Professor Onderdonk . . . [has] been successful." In response, the judge advocate general's office noted, "Onderdonk is said to be in N. Y. City." This small file does not contain anything else, which suggests that the arrest warrant was never carried out, and there are no other records to suggest that Onderdonk or anyone else from the college was ever arrested or charged to appear before a military commission.[8]

Maryland Agricultural College underwent severe financial distress that summer and fall, particularly after its benefactor, Charles Calvert, died. Debts came due, and with the state legislature now involved in the administration of the college's affairs, pressure on Onderdonk mounted to resign his position. Only eight students received their degrees during his tenure, indicating that there were also academic problems at the college during his administration. Even though his three sons were enrolled at the college as students, Onderdonk stepped down from his position as president in the late fall of 1864, his tenure over. The following year, Rev. Libertus Van Bokkelen, who had been Onderdonk's mentor at St. Timothy's Hall, and now serving as the Maryland State School Superintendent, tried to salvage his protégé's reputation. During a June 1865 commencement speech at the college, Van Bokkelen declared, "the success with which [the college] had been maintained under the embarrassing circumstances of the past years, show a degree of vitality which gave assurance of its future growth."[9] A Baltimore newspaper later claimed that Onderdonk had resigned as a consequence of his

8 "Memorandum," found in Case File #4089 in the Turner-Baker Papers, National Archives and Records Administration, Washington, D.C.

9 "Henry Onderdonk," www.flickr.com/photos/digitalcollectionsum/6258589333.

strong Southern sympathies, which undoubtedly played a significant role in his downfall.[10]

After stepping down at the college, Onderdonk settled in Baltimore and opened a successful school there, which he ran for several years. In 1868, he published a textbook on Maryland history that omitted any mention of the how Confederate troops were received during the 1864 invasion of Maryland.[11] In 1870, he released a revised edition of the book that admitted, "A large proportion of the men of this command were Marylanders, and however cold their reception was in the Western part of the State, it cannot be denied that they were cordially received by the farmers of Prince George's County."[12] Those farmers undoubtedly included the faculty and staff of the Maryland Agricultural College.

In 1869, after being asked to do so by Bishop William R. Whittingham, Episcopal bishop of Baltimore, and despite strong misgivings, Onderdonk accepted an appointment as the second headmaster of St. James College in Williamsport, Maryland. He was happy with the success of his school in Baltimore and thought that Williamsport was too remote for his tastes. St. James had been shut down for four years as a consequence of the Civil War a significant portion of the July 6, 1863 Battle of Williamsport during the retreat from Gettysburg was fought on the grounds of the school, and it was located between the lines of the armies for several days before the Army of Northern Virginia finally crossed the Potomac back into what was now West Virginia.[13]

10 "Mr. Henry Onderdonk. "His Funeral and Sketch of His Career as an Educator," *Baltimore Sun*, August 19, 1895,

11 "Henry Onderdonk," www.flickr.com/photos/digitalcollectionsum/ 6258589333.

12 Henry Onderdonk, *A History of Maryland Upon the Basis of McSherry, for the Use of Schools* (Baltimore: John Murphy & Co., 1870), 282-283.

13 For a detailed discussion of the Battle of Williamsport, see Eric J. Wittenberg, J. David Petruzzi and Michael F. Nugent, *One Continuous Fight: The Retreat from Gettysburg and the Pursuit of Robert E. Lee's Army of Northern Virginia, July 4-13, 1863* (El Dorado Hills, CA: Savas Beatie, 2008).

Onderdonk re-opened St. James as a secondary school. When he accepted the appointment as headmaster, the school was in disarray: the school's caretaker had converted one wing into a stable occupied by horses, cattle, and chickens. Much of the campus had been planted with grain crops. He reorganized the school and successfully re-established it, remaining as its headmaster for 27 years and restoring its reputation as a fine educational institution.[14] "This has been successfully conducted down to the present time," noted a Baltimore newspaper in 1895. "He found the place in a state of ruin, and he made it one of the most beautiful places in Maryland."[15]

Onderdonk attended an Episcopal Church convention in Washington, DC in 1894, and took ill there. He managed "to get around the house for about a month before he took to his bed." It was the beginning of his long decline. Onderonk died at age 73 on August 14, 1895 after a three-month illness. His funeral was held at St. John's Episcopal Church in Hagerstown, Maryland, and he was then buried in Green Mount Cemetery in Baltimore. "The funeral was attended by a large number of the leading people of Washington County," declared his obituary in a Baltimore newspaper. He left behind three children from his first marriage and his second wife, Mary, the daughter of Benjamin Latrobe, the famous chief engineer of the Baltimore & Ohio Railroad, and one son.[16]

Thus ended the strange saga of Henry Onderdonk. We will never know whether the cordial greeting extended to Bradley Johnson and his raiders was happenstance and unexpected, or whether the visit had been planned and part of a scheme in which he was involved.

14 "The Late Henry Onderdonk, M.A.," *The Churchman*, Vol. 72 (1895), 266.

15 "Mr. Henry Onderdonk. "His Funeral and Sketch of His Career as an Educator," *Baltimore Sun*, August 19, 1895,

16 Ibid.

Appendix E

Point Lookout Today

By June of 1865, as the last Confederate soldiers were surrendering in the Trans-Mississippi theater, nearly 20,000 prisoners remained jammed into the Point Lookout prison camp in Maryland. The captives were crammed into a space intended to hold half as many when it was constructed in 1863.

Some remained optimistic despite their terrible conditions. "[M]ost things, whether good or bad, will come to an end. More than two months had passed since Lee's surrender. The Confederacy was no more, and then the Federal Government took courage," recounted Virginian Charles T. Loehr, who had been captured at Five Forks on April 1, 1865. "About the middle of June it commenced to release those that were still living, but, in consequence of the inhuman treatment they had received, too feeble to fight again. Then we were duly sworn not to fight them again, to support the Constitution and amendments. Also registering our good looks, weight, height, &c., and getting our signatures made us free men again."[1]

By the time that the last of the Southerners went home, more than 50,000 Confederate prisoners of war had passed through the gates of Point Lookout in the less than two years of its existence. About 3,000 of never returned home. In 1867, the United States

1 Loehr, "Point Lookout," 120.

government sent E. Edward Gilbert, an agent of the U.S. Army's Quartermaster Department, to survey the land at Point Lookout. His job was to consolidate the five scattered cemeteries that housed the bodies of both Union and Confederate dead in anticipation of building a national cemetery. The Confederate remains, the Union soldiers who died at the hospital there, and the contrabands had been commingled throughout the cemeteries. The Union remains were disinterred shortly after the end of the war and moved to Arlington National Cemetery, where they rest to this day. That left the question of what to do with the Confederate remains.

The Southern graves required a great deal of maintenance. Weeds and shifting sands covered many wooden headboards making it difficult to locate some of the graves. Agent Gilbert advised his superiors at the Quartermaster Department that he had problems digging in the loose sand and gravel, which tended to fall back into the holes. This extra work forced him to bury two bodies in one grave. Confederate corpses remained scattered throughout the area.[2]

The Confederate graves were moved several times over the next half-century. One of the larger cemeteries was located just to the north of the enlisted men's prison camp. By 1870, erosion forced the relocation of remains farther inland in the cemetery. They remained there until 1910, when they were moved again to a final resting place a short distance north of the site of the prison camp on Maryland Route 5 near the village of Scotland. The state of Maryland took possession of the cemetery, which is now known as the Point Lookout Confederate Cemetery.

The combination of decomposition and the relocations of the bodies made it impossible to identify individual remains, so 3,004 Confederate soldiers were buried in a mass grave marked by a 25-foot white marble obelisk erected in 1876 by the people of St. Mary's, Calvert, and Charles counties. Inscriptions grace all four sides. The south face reads: "At the call of patriotism and duty they encountered the perils of the field, endured the trials of a prison,

2 Triebe, *Point Lookout Prison Camp and Hospital*, 89.

and were faithful, even unto death." The east face lists the number of deaths at the prison for each state of the Confederacy:

STATE	BURIALS	STATE	BURIALS
Virginia:	640	Mississippi:	42
North Carolina:	962	Florida:	31
South Carolina:	248	Kentucky:	18
Georgia:	249	Texas:	6
Alabama:	75	Maryland:	6
Tennessee:	63	Arkansas:	4
Louisiana:	38	Missouri:	4
Subtotal:			2386
Confederate States Not Designated:			618
Total Burials:			3004[3]

In 1910, Maryland transferred ownership of the Confederate Cemetery to the United States government, which erected an 80-foot granite obelisk to mark the common grave of the Confederate soldiers buried there. The Van Amringe Granite Company of Boston constructed that monument, which was completed in May of 1911.

Twelve bronze tablets were affixed to the monument and were also set around its earthen mount that carry the names and commands of the 3,382 known Confederate sailors and sailors who died at Point Lookout. When the Federal monument was completed, the Maryland state monument was relocated to one of the original prison cemeteries with a bronze plaque that told the history of the

3 Ibid.

move. The state monument was returned to the Point Lookout Confederate Cemetery in 1938 when the federal government sold the other properties. Today, both monuments stand silent guard over the mass grave.[4]

The Point Lookout Confederate Cemetery is located on Maryland Route 5 (Point Lookout Road), roughly two miles south of the village of Scotland, Maryland. The cemetery is open for visitation daily from sunrise to sunset and is overseen by the Baltimore National Cemetery. While visiting, please be mindful that this cemetery is hallowed ground. Please be respectful to the fallen soldiers who rest there.

Little remains of the Point Lookout hospital and prison camp. More than a 150 years of storms and erosion have largely obliterated those sites, which are today mostly under the waters of the Chesapeake Bay. The site is now a Maryland state park of more than 1,000 acres that includes the 1830 lighthouse constructed on Point Lookout. The earthworks associated with Fort Lincoln, the last fortification of the three forts erected for the defense of Point Lookout, remain. Fort Lincoln was the primary Union fortification on Point Lookout, a four-sided earthen fort approximately 60 yards square with embrasures for six cannons, a powder magazine, and a sally port entrance. Loose dirt had been piled on the outside to slow potential attackers, and hardened interiors would resist the impact of artillery fire. At the rear, an L-shaped pass protected the fort's gates from artillery fire or a battering ram. A dry moat surrounded the entire fort. Because of when and where it was built, Fort Lincoln never saw any action.[5]

The barracks and officer quarters of Fort Lincoln have been recreated and a Civil War museum can be found there. What some have surmised to be a surviving earthen redoubt identified by a large depression in the middle of Point Lookout northeast of Fort

4 "Point Lookout Confederate Cemetery, Ridge, Maryland," www.nps.gov/nr/travel/national_cemeteries/maryland/point_lookout_confederate_cemetery.html.

5 "Fort Lincoln Point Lookout, Maryland," www.waymarking.com/waymarks/WM6HQT_Fort_Lincoln_Point_Lookout_Maryland.

Lincoln is in fact a modern dump site for surplus dredging created by the park service. Some of the original grave sites of the Confederate prisoners who died at Point Lookout can still be discerned near the bay side of Point Lookout, and there are a number of interpretive markers that address the sites of interest. What some have assumed to be the only surviving building of the war located at the tip of Point Lookout, is actually a modern smokehouse constructed in the early 1900s used by one of the lighthouse keepers. Beyond that, there are no remaining semblances of either the hospital or prison camp that occupied Point Lookout for the last two years of the Civil War.[6]

Today, Point Lookout is a site where families can enjoy the beauty of nature and the peaceful waters of the Chesapeake Bay and the Potomac River. It bears little or no resemblance to the horrors of the Confederate prisoner of war camp that made the place notorious and claimed the lives of nearly 4,000 Southern soldiers whose earthly remains still fill the Point Lookout Confederate Cemetery.

6 "Point Lookout State Park, Civil War Museum & Lighthouse," www.visitstmarysmd.com/directory/point-lookout-state-park/.

BIBLIOGRAPHY

NEWSPAPERS

Baltimore American
Baltimore County Advocate
Baltimore Sun
Carroll Record
Frank Leslie's Illustrated Newspaper
Harper's Weekly
Herald and Torch Light (Hagerstown, Maryland)
National Daily Republican (Washington, DC)
New York Herald
New York Times
The Harford County Correspondent
The Leader (Laurel, Maryland)
The Valley Spirit (Chambersburg, Pennsylvania)
Washington Evening Star
Worcester Daily Spy

MANUSCRIPT MATERIALS

Special Collections, Connecticut State Library, Hartford, Connecticut:
William B. Franklin Papers

Archives, Huntington Library, San Marino, California:
CW 100 Collection
Jubal Early letter of June 28, 1864

Archives, Maryland Historical Society, Baltimore, Maryland:
Augustus W. Bradford Papers
Harry Gilmor Papers, 1862-1865

National Archives and Records Administration, Washington, DC:

RG 112, War Records, Surgeon General's Office, Letter Book 3
Turner-Baker Papers
Case File #4089, "Henry Onderdonk"

West Virginia State Archives, Charleston, West Virginia:
James E. Sedinger, "Diary of a Border Ranger."

Special Collections, Alderman Library, Univ. of Virginia, Charlottesville, Virginia:
B. T. Holliday, "Account of My Capture."

THESIS

Davis, Lydia Habliston. "Bradley T. Johnson, Brigadier General, C.S.A." Master's Thesis, Virginia Polytechnic and State University, 1973.

PUBLISHED SOURCES

"Affairs in Baltimore; Habeas Corpus Case—Return of the Sheriff—Action of Chief Justice Taney; President's Instructions to Gen. Cadwallader, Suspending the Writ, Etc.," *New York Times*, May 29, 1861.

Basler, Roy, ed. *The Collected Works of Abraham Lincoln.* 9 vols. New Brunswick, NJ: Rutgers University Press, 1953-1955.

Booth, George W. *Personal Reminiscences of a Maryland Soldier in the War Between the States, 1861-1865.* Baltimore: Fleet, McGinley & Co., 1898.

"Bradley Johnston's Pistol," *New York Times,* July 31, 1864,

Butler, Benjamin F. *Private and Personal Correspondence of Gen. Benjamin F. Butler During the Period of the Civil War.* 5 vols. Norwood, MA: Plimpton Press, 1917.

Crist, Linda Laswell, ed. *The Papers of Jefferson Davis.* 14 vols. Baton Rouge: Louisiana State University Press, 1999.

Cullum, George Washington. *Biographical Register of the Officers and Graduates of the U.S. Military Academy at West Point, New York.* 3 vols. New York: D. Van Nostrand, 1868.

"Cutting the Railroads." *Washington Evening Star,* July 11, 1864.

Davis, Erick F., ed. "A Pikesville Diary of 1864." *History Trails* Vol. 13, No. 3 (Spring 1979): 9-13.

Driver, Robert J., Jr. *First & Second Maryland Cavalry, C.S.A.* Charlottesville, VA: Rockbridge Publishing.

Early, Jubal A. *Autobiographical Sketch and Narrative of the War Between the States.* Philadelphia: J. B. Lippincott, 1912.

——. *A Memoir of the Last Year of the War of Independence in the Confederate States of America.* Toronto, Canada: Lovell and Gibson, 1866.

Freeman, Douglas Southall, ed. *Lee's Dispatches.* New York: G. P. Putnam's Sons, 1915.

Gilmor, Harry. *Four Years in the Saddle.* New York: Harper & Bros., 1866.

Goldsborough, William W. *The Maryland Line in the Confederate Army 1861-1865.* Baltimore: Guggenheimer, Weil, and Co., 1900.

Gordon, John B. *Reminiscences of the Civil War.* New York: Charles Scribner's Sons, 1904.

Hard, Abner N. *History of the Eighth Cavalry Regiment Illinois Volunteers, During the Great Rebellion.* Aurora, IL: privately published, 1868.

"Henry Onderdonk." *Herald and Torch Light,* August 22, 1895.

Johnson, Bradley T. "My Ride Around Baltimore in Eighteen Hundred and Sixty-Four." *Southern Historical Society Papers* 30. Richmond: Southern Historical Society, 1902, 215-225.

——. "Riding a Raid in July, 1864." *The Leader,* December 26, 1902.

——. "The Maryland Line." Clement A. Evans, ed. *Confederate Military History.* 12 vols. Atlanta: Confederate Publishing Co., 1899, 2:114-133.

Jones, John B. *A Rebel War Clerk's Diary at the Confederate States Capital.* 2 vols. Philadelphia: J.B. Lippincott and Co., 1866.

Lang, Theodore F. *Loyal West Virginia From 1861 to 1865.* Baltimore, MD: The Deutsch Publishing Co., 1895.146.

Lee, Robert E., Jr. *Recollections and Letters of General Robert E. Lee*. New York: Doubleday, Page & Co., 1904.

Miller, Samuel H., ed. "The Civil War Memoirs of the First Maryland Cavalry, C.S.A., by Henry Clay Mettam." *Maryland Historical Magazine* 58 (1963): 137-169.

"Mr. Henry Onderdonk. His Funeral and Sketch of His Career as an Educator." *Baltimore Sun*, August 19, 1895.

Newcomer, C. Armour. *Cole's Cavalry, or Three Years in the Saddle in the Shenandoah Valley*. Baltimore: Cushing & Co., 1895.

"News from Washington." *New York Herald*, July 8, 1864.

Official Records of the Union and Confederate Navies in the War of the Rebellion. 30 vols. in 2 series. Washington, DC: U. S. Government Printing Office, 1894-1927.

Onderdonk, Henry. *A History of Maryland Upon the Basis of McSherry, for the Use of Schools*. 2nd ed. Baltimore: John Murphy & Co., 1870.

Post, Lydia Mintern, ed. *Soldiers' Letters, From Camp, Battle-Field and Prison*. New York: Bunch & Huntington, 1865.

"Rebels at Magnolia on the Philadelphia, Wilmington & Baltimore." *Valley Spirit*, July 13, 1864.

Reid, Whitelaw. *Ohio in the War: Her Statesmen, Generals, and Soldiers*. 2 vols. Cincinnati: The Robert Clarke Co., 1895.

"Respect to the Memory of the Late Hon. Charles B. Calvert," *Daily National Republican*, May 18, 1864.

Robertson, James I., ed. *Soldier of Southwestern Virginia: The Civil War Letters of Captain John Preston Sheffey*. Baton Rouge: Louisiana State University Press, 2004.

Simon, John Y. ed. *The Papers of Ulysses S. Grant*. 32 vols. Carbondale: Southern Illinois University Press, 1967-2012.

"The Excitement in Baltimore—The Burning of Gunpowder Bridge—Destruction of Gov. Bradford's House—An Act of Retaliation." *New York Times*, July 12, 1864.

"The Invasion of Maryland in 1864." *Frank Leslie's Illustrated Newspaper*, July 30, 1864.

"The Late Henry Onderdonk, M.A." *The Churchman*. Vol. 72 (1895): 266.

"The Magnolia Raid." *New York Times*, July 14, 1864.

"The Raiders.; How Bradley Johnson was Captured and Escaped the Raid in Maryland. Strength of the Rebel Force." *New York Times*, July 19, 1864.

"The Rebel Guerrillas." *New York Times*, July 14, 1864.

The War of the Rebellion: A Compilation of the Official Records of the Union and Confederate Armies. 128 volumes in 3 series. Washington, DC: United States Government Printing Office, 1889.

Thompson, Magnus S. "Plant to Release Our Men at Point Lookout." *Confederate Veteran* 20 (1912): 69-70.

"Value and Economy of the Veteran Reserve Corps," *New York Times*, October 6, 1865.

Wells, James T. "Prison Experience," *Southern Historical Society Papers* 7 (July 1879): 324-330.

Wild, Frederick W. *Memoirs and History of Capt. F. W. Alexander's Baltimore Battery of Light Artillery U.S.V.* Baltimore: Press of the Maryland School for Boys, 1912.

SECONDARY SOURCES

Ackinclose, Timothy. *Sabres & Pistols: The Civil War Career of Colonel Harry Gilmor, C.S.A.: The Civil War Career of Colonel Harry Gilmor, C.S.A.* Baltimore: Butternut & Blue, 1997.

Baron, Richard, Abe Baum, and Richard Goldhurst. *Raid! The Untold Story of Patton's Secret Mission.* New York: Random House, 1981.

Beitzel, Edwin W. *Point Lookout Prison Camp for Confederates.* Leonardtown, MD: St. Mary's Historical Society, 1983.

Brooks, Neal A. and Erlc G. Rockel. *A History of Baltimore County.* Towson, MD: Friends of the Towson Library, Inc., 1979.

Cooling, Benjamin Franklin, III. *Jubal Early: Robert E. Lee's Bad Old Man.* New York: Rowman & Littlefield, 2014.

——. *Jubal Early's Raid on Washington 1864.* Mt. Pleasant, SC: Nautical & Aviation Publishing Co., 1989.

DeBoalt, Katherine Drew. "Once There was a Castle." *Baltimore Sun*, June 6, 1993.

Dickinson, Jack L. *8th Virginia Cavalry.* Lynchburg, VA: H. E. Howard, 1986.

Driver, Robert J., Jr, *First and Second Maryland Cavalry.* Charlottesville, VA: Rockbridge Publishing, 1999.

Duncan, Richard R. "Maryland's Reaction to Early's Raid in 1864: A Summer of Bitterness." *Maryland Historical Magazine*, Vol. 64, No. 3 (Fall 1969): 248-279.

Gallagher, Gary W. "Jubal Anderson Early." William C. Davis and Julie Hoffman, eds. *The Confederate General.* 6 vols. New York: National Historical Society, 1991, 2:88-91.

Gottfried, Bradley M. and Linda I. Gottfried. *Hell Comes to Southern Maryland: The Story of Point Lookout Prison and Hammond General Hospital.* Fairfield, PA: Turning Point Publishing, 2018.

Hanson, George A. *Old Kent: The Eastern Shore of Maryland.* Baltimore: George P. DesForges, 1876.

Hiebert, Ray Eldon and Richard K. McMaster. *A Grateful Remembrance: The Story of Montgomery County, Maryland*, Rockville, MD: Montgomery County Historical Society, 1976.

Judge, Joseph. *Season of Fire: The Confederate Strike on Washington.* Charlottesville, VA: Rockbridge Press, 1994.

Klein, Frederic Shriver, ed. *Just South of Gettysburg.* Westminster, MD: Carroll County Historical Society, 1963.

Krick, Robert K. *Lee's Colonels: A Biographical Register of the Field Officers of the Army of Northern Virginia.* 4th ed. Dayton, OH: Morningside House, 1992.

Loeffelbein, Robert L. "Point Lookout Prison: The Truth Beneath the Ruins." *Maryland Magazine* (Spring 1982): 12-14.

Mathews, Byron H., Jr. *The McCook-Stoneman Raid.* Philadelphia: Dorrance & Co., 1976.

Michel, Robert E. *Colonel Harry Gilmor's Raid Around Baltimore.* Baltimore: Erbe Publishers, 1976.

Mingus, Scott. *Soldiers, Spies & Steam: A History of the Northern Central Railway in the Civil War.* Scotts Valley, CA: Createspace, 2016.

Mingus, Scott L., Sr. and Robert L. Williams. *"This Trying Hour": The Philadelphia, Wilmington & Baltimore Railroad in the Civil War.* Scotts Valley, CA: Makespace, 2017.

Nelson, Robert H. and Emma L. Nelson. *James M. Corns: The Ancestry and Life of a Warrior.* Denver, CO: Outskirts Press, 2010.

Newman, Harry Wright. *Maryland and the Confederacy.* Annapolis, MD: privately published, 1976.

Patchan, Scott C. *Shenandoah Summer: The 1864 Valley Campaign.* Lincoln: University of Nebraska Press, 2007.

——. *The Battle of Piedmont and Hunter's Raid on Staunton: The 1864 Shenandoah Campaign.* Charleston, SC: The History Press, 2011.

Sander, Kathleen Waters. *John W. Garrett and the Baltimore & Ohio Railroad.* Baltimore, MD: Johns Hopkins University Press, 2017.

Schwartz, Charles S. "John Taylor Wood: Confederate Commando." *Military Images* 2 (July-August 1980): 4-5.

Scott, J. L. *36th and 37th Battalions Virginia Cavalry.* Lynchburg, VA: H. E. Howard, 1986.

Sheads, Scott Sumpter and Daniel Carroll Toomey. *Baltimore During the Civil War.* Linthicum, MD: Toomey Press, 1997.

Shingleton, Royce G. *John Taylor Wood: Sea Ghost of the Confederacy.* Athens: University of Georgia Press, 1979.

Snell, Mark A. *From First to Last: The Life of William B. Franklin.* New York: Fordham University Press, 2002.

Stephens, Gail. *Shadow of Shiloh: Major General Lew Wallace in the Civil War.* Indianapolis: Indiana Historical Society, 2010.

Tidwell, William H., James O. Hall and David Winfred Gaddy. *Come Retribution: The Confederate Secret Service and the Assassination of President Lincoln.* Jackson, MS: University of Mississippi Press, 1988.

Toomey, Daniel Carroll. *The Civil War in Maryland.* Baltimore: Toomey Press, 1983.

Triebe, Richard H. *Point Lookout Prison Camp and Hospital: The North's Largest Civil War Prison.* Middletown, DE: Coastal Books, 2014.

Venter, Bruce M. *Kill Jeff Davis: The Union Raid on Richmond, 1864.* Norman: University of Oklahoma Press, 2016.

Warner, Ezra J. *Generals in Blue: Lives of the Union Commanders.* Baton Rouge: Louisiana State University, 1964.

Warner, Nancy M, Ralph B. Levering, and Margaret Taylor Woltz. *Carroll County Maryland: A History 1837-1976.* Westminster, MD: Carroll County Bicentennial Committee, 1976.

Wert, Jeffry D. "Bradley Tyler Johnson." William C. Davis and Julie Hoffman, eds. *The Confederate General.* 6 vols. National Historical Society, 1991, 3:172-179.

——. *From Winchester to Cedar Creek: The Shenandoah Campaign of 1864.* Carlisle, PA: South Mountain Press, 1987.

——. "George Washington Custis Lee." William C. Davis and Julie Hoffman, eds. *The Confederate General.* 6 vols. National Historical Society, 1991, 4:42-43.

——. "Robert Ransom, Jr." William C. Davis and Julie Hoffman, eds. *The Confederate General.* 6 vols. National Historical Society, 1991, 5:80-81.

WEBSITES

"Henry Onderdonk." Www.flickr.com/photos/digitalcollectionsum/6258589333.

"History of the Gunpowder River." www.greatfeathers.com/overview-history-maryland.

"Timeline: The University of Maryland." www.umd.edu/history-and-mission/timeline.

"John Lee Carroll," Archives of Maryland Biographical Series. https://msa.maryland.gov/megafile/msa/speccol/sc3500/sc3520/001400/001468/html/1468extbio.html.

Smith, Ellen Oliver. "The Magnolia Station Train Raid." Www.madonna.Edu/pages/mmtrain.cfm.

INDEX

About the Author

Eric J. Wittenberg is an accomplished American Civil War cavalry historian and author. The Ohio attorney has authored nearly two dozen books on various Civil War subjects, with particular focus on cavalry operations, as well as three dozen articles in popular magazines. His first book, *Gettysburg's Forgotten Cavalry Actions*, won the prestigious 1998 Bachelder-Coddington Literary Award, as did his recent 2022 book (with Scott L. Mingus Sr.) *"If We Are Striking for Pennsylvania": The Army of Northern Virginia and Army of the Potomac March to Gettysburg, Vol. 1: June 3-21, 1863*. His 2014 *"The Devil's to Pay": John Buford at Gettysburg. A History and Walking Tour*, was awarded the Gettysburg Civil War Roundtable's 2015 Book Award. Wittenberg is a popular speaker on the Civil War circuit and an active preservationist. He lives in Columbus with his wife Susan and their beloved dogs.